OCD

A Workbook for Clinicians, Children & Teens

Actions to Beat, Control & Defeat
Obsessive Compulsive Disorder

Christina J. Taylor, Ph.D.

Copyright © 2016 by Christina J. Taylor, PhD

Published by
PESI Publishing & Media
PESI, Inc
3839 White Ave
Eau Claire, WI 54703

Cover: Amy Rubenzer
Editing: Marietta Whittlesey
Layout: Bookmasters & Amy Rubenzer

ISBN: 9781559570503

Printed in the United States of America.

PESI
Publishing
& Media
www.pesipublishing.com

"Do you want to beat, control and defeat OCD? Dr. Taylor shows how children and teens can do exactly that. Her optimism for their recovery shines through as she demonstrates how they can take on the "OCD Trickster" and eliminate the OCD symptoms that disrupt their lives. Using the metaphor of a "fear rocket" for how obsessions and compulsions skyrocket out of control, she teaches how to ride it "to a safe landing," by managing the fear that drives OCD. With vivid examples of symptoms such as checking, scary thoughts and contamination, Dr. Taylor describes the ABCD's of eliminating them, providing easy-to-use worksheets for effective exposure and response prevention plans. This is a must-read for anyone who wants to help the young people in their lives recover from OCD!"

-**Margaret Wehrenberg, PsyD**
Author of *The 10 Best-Ever Anxiety
Treatment Techniques*

"I'm so pleased that Christina has written this wonderful book. With her extensive experience treating folks with OCD, Christina is well respected by experts in the field and most importantly by those whom she treats for this difficult illness. This book with its easy to follow concepts, illustrations and charts, will be so helpful to many people. Behavior therapy techniques helps many feel more in control of their symptoms and their lives, and Christina has made these techniques accessible in her book. It is sure to become a resource for them to continually refer to over time."

-**Suzanne Wasylink, RN-BC**
Yale OCD Research Clinic

"Dr. Taylor has surely written one of the more comprehensive books for childhood OCD. It is a welcome addition to an area that still lacks adequate materials. It is chock full of helpful and proven approaches and materials, and I'm sure that it will be of great help to the many clinicians, parents, and children out there who do their best each day to cope with this serious and chronic problem."

-**Fred Penzel, PhD**
Licensed Psychologist and Executive
Director of Western Suffolk Psychological Services

"Dr. Taylor's well researched and sensitively written workbook on Obsessive Compulsive Disorder has elevated the dialogue and extended the knowledge about this challenging disorder. The integration of the current information on both theory and treatment means that clients and clinicians alike can now improve recovery and management of OCD. The many new strategies and treatment options for clients will dispel the myths about OCD and reduce the worry that families and clinicians experience when trying to be of help to those affected. It's comprehensive and of value to clients, families, and clinicians. It's engaging and optimistic in its presentation, so it is easy to read and understand. I would recommend it to anyone who wants to be a better therapist, support person, or friend to those impacted by this condition."

-**Ruth M. Grant, PhD**
Sacred Heart University

"Christina J. Taylor's *OCD: A Workbook for Clinicians, Children & Teens* will be the professionals' newest go-to workbook for treating OCD, and is an ideal resource for children, adolescents and their parents. What's new about this workbook is the content, description and treatment of the obsessional aspects of OCD. The rhythm of the text and the clever worksheets carry the reader along in learning how to take Actions to Beat, Control & Defeat OCD."

-Diane E. Sholomskas, PhD
Psychologist, Center for Anxiety Disorders & Phobias
Volunteer Faculty, Yale University School of Medicine

"Dr. Taylor's OCD workbook is exceptionally well written and thorough, explaining the wide and varied symptoms of OCD and how the disorder affects daily life as a child or teen. This book is a timely resource for parents and caregivers and allows children and teens to actively manage symptoms and improve their quality of life. It provides the framework and support that families need to beat, control and defeat OCD, no matter how daunting the task may be. The worksheets are invaluable and allow clinicians and families to develop a plan that can be implemented gradually and steadily. This ensures that strength is gained, successes are attained and that the team works together to defeat OCD. As a parent of a young adult with OCD, I highly recommend this book."

-Susan Schuster, PT, DPT
President of OCD Connecticut

**To my parents,
Anastasia & Ernest, and Sara**

Acknowledgements

I have a profound debt of gratitude to each and every one of the children, adolescents, and adults who came to me for help with their OCD over the last twenty-five years. Your willingness to engage your OCD has taught me invaluable lessons about resilience, bravery, perseverance, humor, kindness, and compassion in dealing with the struggles of life.

I am especially thankful to Patricia Perkins Doyle and Susan Duffy for their pioneering work on behalf of the Obsessive Compulsive Foundation. The encouragement, friendship, and support that they provided in those early years of my practice were especially vital to me personally and professionally. The spirited support group meetings that led into the late hours of the night in that lovely brick building in Milford, Connecticut were truly inspirational. The ongoing success of the Fairfield County OCD Support Group is a tribute to their foundational work. I have a special appreciation for my long collaboration with Dr. Diane E. Sholomskas, whose expertise and loyal friendship has been a true gift in my life.

I also want to give special thanks to the Connecticut people who have contributed so much to the work on treatments for OCD –Dr. Christopher Pittenger and Suzanne Wasylink, R.N. at the Yale OCD Research Clinic, Susan Schuster, founder of OCD Connecticut, the members of the Fairfield County OCD Support Group, and Rocco Clericuzio, our expert and dedicated webmaster!

Finally, thanks to all the editors at PESI for their assiduous support, adept editing, and creative design in the publication of my work.

Table of Contents

Introduction

I had the good fortune to learn cognitive behavior therapy (CBT) for treating Obsessive-Compulsive Disorder (OCD) in my post-doctoral internship with Dr. Fugen Neziroglu, clinical director of the Biobehavioral Institute in Great Neck, New York, and a leading expert on OCD. Dr. Fred Penzel, a renowned expert on the treatment of OCD, was also serendipitously on the staff of the Biobehavioral Institute during the time of my training. The superlative clinical training I received set me on a path to provide expert treatment for obsessive-compulsive disorder–truly rewarding work that I have been doing over the last 25 years. While exposure and response prevention (ERP) was established at the time of my training as the gold standard for the treatment of OCD in adults, there was very little information in the 1990's about how to apply ERP treatment to children. Clinicians working with children were faced with figuring out for themselves how to adapt ERP strategies for young clients. As it turned out, those of us who used ERP with kids in clinical practice found that it worked; indeed, sometimes it appeared to work even better with kids than with adults!

Numerous controlled research trials have since shown that exposure-based CBT for OCD is very effective with children 7 to 17 years of age (Abramowitz et al., 2005; Franklin et al., 2011; Freeman et al., 2014; Storch et al., 2010; Torp et al., 2015). CBT has been established as the first line treatment for children and adolescents with mild to moderate symptoms of OCD, a majority of them (65% - 80%) showing improvement with treatment. A selective serotonin inhibiting medication (SSRI) can be added later if necessary to achieve greater amelioration of the child's symptoms. For those who enter treatment with more severe symptoms, or who are hesitant about tackling their OCD, or who have co-occurring disorders, a combination of CBT and an SSRI can be employed from the outset. Importantly, the research shows that **CBT is more effective than medication alone for treating children, and the improvements achieved through CBT are longer-lasting than those obtained through medication alone.** This finding is consistent with research on adults that shows a high rate of relapse when medication is discontinued without having engaged in CBT for OCD.

While the clinical research points to the efficacy of CBT for treating OCD, the reality is that many clinicians in the community do not use exposure-based CBT for treating OCD. This is so despite the fact that qualified mental health professionals are capable of providing this empirically based therapy to their young clients. *OCD: A Workbook for Clinicians, Children & Teens* provides you with all the tools you need to do so. It is a comprehensive, clinically sound, user-friendly, and creative guide to CBT for OCD. It reflects the American Academy of Child and Adolescent Psychiatry (AACAP) guidelines for the treatment of pediatric OCD (Geller & March, 2012). **Clinicians can use *OCD: A Workbook for Clinicians, Children & Teens* with young clients as well as their parents, relatives, and teachers. The techniques explained in the workbook are actually also appropriate for adults given the fact that the basic principles of treatment for OCD are the same for children and adults.**

The need for clinicians in the community to use these evidence-based tools is underscored by the following:

- OCD is estimated to affect over one million children and adolescents in the United States.

- OCD commonly appears between 7 to 12 years of age, although it can appear at much younger ages.

- Boys have an earlier onset of OCD than girls.

- The majority of adults with OCD report that they experienced obsessive-compulsive symptoms in their childhood.

- The symptoms of childhood OCD are similar to those of adults.

- On average two or more years can elapse between the onset of symptoms and beginning CBT treatment.

- If left untreated, the symptoms of OCD grow worse.

These facts show that clinicians in the community are likely to encounter kids and teens who need treatment for OCD. **This workbook offers you, your clients, their families, and their teachers, an opportunity to work collaboratively in learning how to use cognitive-behavioral strategies.** First, the book helps you to enlist children in their own treatment by conveying a message of hope that they can successfully beat OCD through the CBT strategies presented in the book (The ABCDs). Secondly, the book offers a clear explanation and illustration of the OCD vicious circle. This is the foundation for carrying out cognitive behavioral treatment. Throughout my years of working with children and their parents, I have seen the palpable relief felt by children and their parents once they understand the psychological model of OCD and how it can be treated.

A creative metaphor, The Fear Rocket, is used to explain how to break out of the vicious circle. Children envision themselves successfully beating OCD by flying the Fear Rocket until it comes in for a safe landing. When OCD blasts the Fear Rocket into the sky, doing a compulsion is like ejecting from the Fear Rocket and giving power and fuel to the OCD. Staying in the Fear Rocket until it comes down is shown to take longer, but helps them to fly away from OCD to a safe and controlled landing! The Fear Rocket metaphor explains the concept of habituation and serves as the basis for creating an anxiety hierarchy and exposure and response prevention exercises.

Thirdly, The ABCDs of OCD is organized so that young people can easily find themselves in the descriptions and examples of obsessive-compulsive symptoms. Separate chapters explain how CBT techniques can be applied to the major sub-types of OCD – contamination, checking, perfectionism, hoarding, worrisome thoughts, and religious/moral OCD. This is a useful organization for clinicians because it enables you to focus the cognitive-behavioral techniques on the child's specific symptoms.

In sum, all the tools clinicians need for carrying out successful exposure and response prevention are explained in creative and developmentally appropriate ways. **By employing the workbook you will be able to design exposure exercises, practice the exercises in-session, teach cognitive restructuring and anxiety management techniques, and engage families in support of their child's treatment.** *OCD: A Workbook for Clinicians, Children & Teens* offers numerous charts and worksheets for you to engage clients actively in treatment.

Therapist Guide

Chapter 1 – Diagnosis and Psychoeducation

The first step in treating children and adolescents with OCD is to make a diagnosis based on the diagnostic criteria in the *Diagnostic and Statistical Manual of Mental Disorders-5* (DSM-5). The material in Chapter 1 is designed to help clinicians engage the child or teen in beginning to identify obsessive-compulsive symptoms. Examples of obsessions and compulsions experienced by children and teens are presented in A to Z fashion to illustrate sub-types of OCD. Talking about these examples and the nature of obsessions and compulsions can help to validate the child's or teen's experience, opening the door for them to talk about them, sometimes for the first time. As therapy progresses and clients become more knowledgeable about OCD, they are likely to report additional obsessions and compulsions (Chapter 3 provides an opportunity for further assessment). Importantly, parents and caretakers should also be involved in this assessment process from the outset. Children, teens, and parents can provide information about symptoms via the clinician administered Children's Yale-Brown Obsessive Compulsive Scale (CYBOCS) that is cited in the references (Scahill et al., 1997). This measure provides an extensive list of symptoms and a clinical severity score.

It should be noted that the assessment process is, in and of itself, an important step in building rapport with young clients. As treatment of children and teens will of necessity include families, it is important to educate the family about OCD and to assess their involvement in the child's symptoms. Clinicians also need to take into account the presence of comorbid disorders. Comorbid illnesses are common in children with OCD, including depression, Tourette's, ADHD, separation anxiety disorder, specific phobia, social anxiety disorder, and disruptive behavior disorder. The presence of comorbid conditions may necessitate a psychiatric referral and treating these disorders first or along with the OCD. Finally, Chapter 1 offers an opportunity for teaching about the basics of OCD. Obsessions and compulsions are defined and OCD is explained as a worry disorder caused by a chemical imbalance in the brain. OCD is characterized as a Trickster and Fake Out Artist who makes people worry and do unnecessary rituals. Normal worries are distinguished from OCD worries and superstitions. The idea that OCD can be controlled by the ABCDs (Actions to Beat, Control, and Defeat OCD) is introduced. It is very important for you to deliver this message of hope to reinforce treatment readiness and motivation.

Chapter 2 – Understanding OCD: Knowledge is Power

Chapter 2 provides clinicians with a child and teen friendly explanation of the psychological model for understanding OCD. OCD is depicted as a trickster who bullies people into carrying out unnecessary compulsions that traps them in a vicious circle. Give the client an opportunity to put a personal stamp on the fight against OCD by giving it a nickname, thereby externalizing the OCD as the target to control. Using behavior therapy – exposure and response prevention – to break out of the OCD vicious circle is explained. A Fear Rocket motif is used to explain the concept of habituation – obsessions cause the Fear Rocket to go high into the sky – doing the compulsion is pictured as a person ejecting or jumping out from the Rocket to get back down to earth. This fuels the OCD, making it stronger. Learning to fly the Fear Rocket means riding in the rocket to a safe landing by not doing a compulsion – it takes longer for the fear to come down but it makes the flyer stronger and the OCD weaker. Illustrations show that flying the Fear Rocket through clouds of worry and fear is the way to beat OCD. The *Learn to Beat, Control and Defeat OCD Yourself* worksheet gives clinicians an opportunity to guide young clients in how to apply the OCD model to their own experience, an important step in teaching them the ABCDs.

Chapter 3 –ABCDs to Beat OCD – Behavior Therapy

The process and steps involved in doing exposure and response prevention are outlined. A detailed list of obsessions and compulsions is presented to help further identify your client's obsessions and compulsions. The list of obsessions includes: contamination, ordering and arranging, collecting and hoarding, perfectionism, harming, illness and safety, moral and religious, doubting, and a miscellaneous category. The compulsions identified are: cleaning and washing, checking, repeating, counting, arranging, saving, collecting and hoarding, religious and moral, avoidance, and other. Asking clients and their parents to keep a daily journal or diary (the forms are provided) is recommended as a tool for identifying obsessions, compulsions, and the triggers that set them off. The Fear Rocket (shown in a graphic) is used to rate the obsessive-compulsive symptoms and arrange them into an anxiety hierarchy (use the form provided). The anxiety hierarchy is described as the road map for doing exposure and response prevention (ERP), beginning with the easiest items and moving up the list in a step-by-step fashion to the highest items. A checklist that details the ABCDs learned to date is provided to review with your client.

Chapter 4 – ABCDs of Coping with Fear

Exposure and Response Prevention is shown to depend on learning to resist the compulsions by steering the Fear Rocket and flying it to a safe landing. Emphasize that it is through repetition that this becomes easier and easier to do because with repetition the Fear Rocket (the fear and worry) doesn't go up as high. The following techniques for carrying out successful exposure and response prevention exercises are explained in detail: 1) Change the compulsion a little and change it again; 2) Reward yourself; 3) Talk to yourself; 4) Talk to the OCD Trickster; 5) Watch out for the Trickster; 6) Rehearse ERP exercises; 7) Say the fear and get it out of your head; 8) Sing your obsession; 9) Record your fear and listen to it; 10) Do the opposite of the compulsion; 11) Exaggerate the obsession; 12) Distraction; 13) Delay or postpone compulsions; 14) Make an appointment with the obsession; 15) Set a time limit on compulsions; 16) Practice not avoiding; 17) Think about your friends; 18) Get a helper; 19) Find a support group; 20) Learn to manage fear and worry through relaxation exercises, including visualization, deep muscle relaxation, and deep breathing. In addition, it is recommended that clinicians and parents design a contingency management program to provide rewards for the child's work on the ABCDs. Teens and adults can benefit from such a plan as well!

Chapter 5 – ABCDs of Fearful Thinking

The basic techniques of cognitive restructuring are explained in language appropriate for children and adolescents. Clinicians should be cognizant of the fact that these are considered adjunctive techniques to exposure-based techniques. How a person thinks is shown to make OCD better or worse. Ten common errors in thinking are described: overestimating, over responsibility, catastrophizing, filtering, shoulds, superstitious or magical thinking, black and white thinking, fortune telling, mind reading, and thought action fusion. Tools and worksheets for identifying and changing thinking errors are provided:
1) Testing and revising thinking – countering overestimations by looking at facts or evidence;
2) Action Experiments – carrying out experiments to test thoughts and predictions; 3) Standing up to Bad Outcomes – learning that you can deal with situations that don't go your way; and 4) Slicing The Pie – developing a more realistic way to think about the causes and responsibility for events. These tools to develop realistic thinking are applied to the type of obsessions and compulsions addressed in each of the chapters that follow.

Applying ABCDs to The Specific Sub-types of OCD

Chapters 6 through 11 are set up for clinicians to guide clients in the use of the ABCDs to tackle each of the major subtypes of OCD. Each chapter contains: (1) Short stories about children with the particular type of obsessive-compulsive symptoms; (2) A detailed list of the most common obsessions and compulsions associated with the subtype; (3) A list of feared consequences associated with the subtype; (4) An illustration of the Vicious Circle; (5) A detailed example of how to use The ABCDs for the specific subtype; and (6) Worksheets for constructing an anxiety hierarchy, identifying the vicious circle, and doing cognitive restructuring.

Chapter 6 – ABCDs for Contamination OCD

Personal stories illustrating different types of contamination obsessions and compulsions are presented. A list of the large variety of common obsessions and compulsions helps clinicians to identify the ones their clients are experiencing: 1) Body products and parts; 2) Natural environment; 3) Environmental contaminants; 4) People – e.g., those who are seen as sick, poor, different, etc.; 5) Animals and animal products; 7) Places and locations – public places, restrooms, cemeteries, towns, etc.; 8) Objects, pictures, words, images – e.g., money, library books, mail, etc. The list of decontamination compulsions includes: 1) Washing; 2) Cleaning; 3) Ritualized washing and cleaning; 4) Throwing things away; 5) Changing clothes; 6) Avoidance; 7) Magical compulsions – e.g., special numbers, words, images, etc. 8) Wearing protective clothing or gear; 9) Reassurance-seeking; 10) Protection of others – e.g., using any decontaminating compulsions. The types of feared consequences linked to contamination OCD are explained as: 1) Physical harm; 2) Psychological/social harm; 3) Spiritual harm; 4) General uneasiness. The lists of contamination obsessions and compulsions and of feared consequences are used to help clients create their anxiety hierarchy and carry out exposure exercises. Illustrations engage clients in envisioning how to break out of the contamination vicious circle. A detailed example of exposure exercises carried out by one boy is described. Cognitive restructuring examples and forms to assist in ERP are also provided.

Chapter 7 – ABCDs for Checking OCD

Personal stories illustrating different types of checking obsessions and compulsions are presented. A list of common checking obsessions and compulsions focused on harm, danger, and safety are explained. Checking obsessions include: 1) Fear of harm by physical, psychological, emotional, spiritual injury, suffering, or pain; 2) Fear of causing physical, psychological, emotional, or spiritual injury, suffering, or pain to others; 3) Fear of harming animals; 4) Fear of damaging your own property or belongings; 5) Fear of damaging other people's property or belongings.

Checking compulsions are identified as: 1) Checking to prevent harm to yourself; 2) Checking to prevent harm to others, or to reassure yourself that no harm was done; 3) Checking to prevent harm to animals, or to reassure yourself that no harm was done; 4) Checking to prevent harm to property, or to reassure yourself that no harm occurred; 5) Checking to prevent harm to others' property or to reassure yourself that no harm occurred; 6) Checking to make sure that something was completed or that it was done correctly, or that it is fully understood.

The feared consequences that drive checking are explained as: 1) Fear of punishment; 2) Fear of self-blame or guilt; 3) Fear of social disapproval; 4) Fear of spiritual harm; 5) Fear of seeing oneself negatively (e.g., a loser, stupid, crazy). The lists of checking obsessions-compulsions and feared consequences set the stage for clients to create their anxiety hierarchy and carry out exposure exercises.

Illustrations engage clients in envisioning how to break out of the checking vicious circle. A detailed example of exposure exercises for checking is described and cognitive restructuring examples and forms for changing thoughts about checking are provided.

Chapter 8 – ABCDs for Perfectionism OCD

Personal stories illustrating perfectionism obsessions and compulsions are presented. Perfectionism OCD is described as trying to meet unrealistic high standards that are impossible to fulfill. The list of perfectionism obsessions helps clients identify what they are experiencing: 1) Overconcern about yourself – hygiene, grooming, clothes, etc.; 2) Overconcern about your performance – speech, writing, grades, athletics, popularity; 3) Overconcern about belongings – preserving things as new, protecting things from damage or normal wear and tear; 4) Overconcern about your environment – order, neatness, balance, or organization.

Perfectionism compulsions are identified as: 1) Slowness; 2) Checking – repeatedly going over actions, work, or performance to make sure there are no errors; 3) Redoing – erasing, crossing out, rewriting, retyping; 4) Repeating – carrying out actions over and over until they are correct or feel right; 5) Reassurance-seeking – repeatedly asking others to review your work, performance, or understanding to make sure it is correct and free from error; 6) Procrastination – delaying or postponing doing tasks because of worry about not doing well or failing.

The feared consequences linked to perfectionism OCD are described as: 1) Negative self-evaluation – seeing yourself as a failure, unworthy, defective, unfit, or incompetent; 2) Negative evaluation by others – being criticized, reprimanded, or rated poorly; 3) Social Rejection – being viewed as unattractive, unfit, or socially unskilled; 4) Feeling uncomfortable – feeling out of control, unable to act, or unable to stop doing compulsive behavior. The lists of perfectionism obsessions-compulsions and feared consequences assist clients to create their anxiety hierarchy and carry out exposure exercises. Illustrations engage clients in envisioning how to break out of the perfectionism vicious circle. A detailed example of exposure exercises for perfectionism is described along with cognitive restructuring examples and forms for changing thoughts about perfectionism.

Chapter 9 – ABCDs for Hoarding OCD

Personal stories illustrating hoarding OCD are presented. Hoarding OCD is defined as collecting and saving worthless, useless, or too many objects. People with hoarding obsessions and compulsions have great difficulty discarding things, and are overly worried about losing or misplacing the things that they have saved. The list of hoarding obsessions includes: 1) Worry about having or getting certain things or possessions; 2) Worry about losing or misplacing things or possessions; 3) Worry about throwing things or possessions away; 4) Worry about anyone moving, using, touching your things or possessions; 5) Worry about spending money appropriately.

Hoarding compulsions are identified as: 1) Collecting or saving an excessive number of objects that interferes with normal living; 2) Collecting or saving worthless or useless objects; 3) Difficulty throwing worthless or useless objects away; 4) Difficulty sharing or allowing others to handle or touch possessions; and 5) Difficulty spending money appropriately.

The feared consequences linked to hoarding are explained as: 1) Feeling uncomfortable, unhappy, angry, and upset; 2) Feeling that part of yourself will be lost; 3) Worry that you won't be able to forget about the lost, misplaced, or discarded possessions; 4) Worry that you won't have things, information, or money that you needs; 5) Worry that you or your family could be hurt; 6) Worry that your things or possessions will be damaged; and 7) Worry that things or possessions will feel bad, hurt, or disappointed.

The lists of hoarding obsessions-compulsions and feared consequences assist clients to create their anxiety hierarchy and carry out exposure exercises. Illustrations engage readers in envisioning how to break out of the hoarding vicious circle. A detailed example of exposure exercises for hoarding is described along with cognitive restructuring examples and forms for changing thoughts about hoarding.

Chapter 10 – ABCDs for Worrisome Thoughts

Worrisome thoughts OCD is described as involving unrealistic thoughts about bad things such as accidents, injuries, illness, violence, sexual conduct, or offensive actions. These thoughts are misinterpreted to mean that the person is bad for having the thoughts, that the thoughts are true, or that they might actually act out the thought. The personal stories about worrisome thoughts describe worries about a parent being hurt in an accident, worry about hurting others, and worry about inappropriate sexual conduct. Worrisome thought obsessions are described as worry about: 1) People or pets having accidents; 2) People or pets being injured or killed; 3) People or pets getting sick or dying; 4) Acting aggressively, harming others or harming animals; 5) Acting out sexually; 6) Inappropriate sexual behavior; 7) Damaging property; 8) Hurting yourself; 9) Killing yourself; 10) Being gay; 11) Saying or doing something inappropriate; 12) Loss of control; 13) Disliking or hating someone.

The list of worrisome thought compulsions includes: 1) Avoidance of people, places, or things; 2) Avoidance of the thought; 3) Picturing pleasant images or thinking happy thoughts; 4) Blocking the thought by using special phrases or numbers; 5) Washing, showering, or cleaning; 6) Repeating actions; 7) Performing ritualized actions; 8) Praying; 9) Checking; 10) Asking for reassurance; 11) Giving oneself reassurance; 12) Testing yourself to make sure the thought is not true; 13) Searching for reassuring information.

The feared consequences associated with worrisome thoughts OCD are identified as: 1) Viewing oneself negatively – seeing oneself as bad, evil, unworthy, etc.; 2) Guilt; 3) Social Disapproval; 4) Punishment; 5) Loss of control – acting out inappropriate urges. A detailed example of a girl with worrisome thoughts about being gay is presented to help clients develop their anxiety hierarchy and exposure exercises. Cognitive restructuring examples and forms are provided to help clients work on changing unrealistic thinking about worrisome thoughts.

Chapter 11 – ABCDs for Worries about Religion, God, and Sin

Religious OCD is defined as overconcern with prayer, God, religious practices, or excessive worry about sin and punishment. Personal stories illustrating different types of religious OCD are presented. Obsessions about God, sin and religion are described as overconcern with: 1) Sin and morality; 2) Inappropriate or embarrassing thoughts; 3) Religious rituals or practices; 4) Virtuous behavior; and 5) Superstitious or magical beliefs. The list of compulsions about religion, God, and sin is described as: 1) Avoidance – e.g., going to church because of fear about praying perfectly; 2) Praying or worshiping compulsively; 3) Repeating; 4) Undoing; 5) Reassurance-seeking; 6) Checking for harm; 7) Confessing; 8) Forgiveness-seeking; 9) Self-denial; 10) Washing or cleaning.

The feared consequences associated with religious OCD are: 1) Punishment by God; 2) Harm caused by the devil; 3) Viewing the self negatively; and 4) Feeling uncomfortable. A detailed example of religious OCD is presented to help clients design their own hierarchy and exposure exercises. An example of cognitive restructuring for religious OCD is presented along with forms for work on changing unrealistic thinking about God, sin, religion, and morality.

Chapter 12 – Working on Scary Obsessions and Compulsions

Techniques for doing exposure and response prevention exercises when tackling obsessions and compulsions at the top of the anxiety hierarchy are explained. Small step exposure plans involve taking difficult items and breaking them down into less anxiety- producing exposures arranged in a new anxiety hierarchy. Examples of small step exposure plans illustrate how to break out tougher exposure exercises into a series of easier more doable steps for your clients. Additional techniques such as carrying out action experiments to test unrealistic predictions are also offered as a technique to help tackling the obsessions and compulsions at the top of the anxiety hierarchy. Worksheets are provided to develop exposure exercises.

Chapter 13 – After you Beat, Control and Defeat OCD!

The importance of continuing to watch out for the return of obsessions and compulsions is explained. Reviewing all the cognitive behavioral skills with clients is important because obsessions and compulsions are likely to reoccur. Keeping skills sharp and at the ready is shown to be the way to successfully manage and control OCD. To help with this, the essential Actions to Beat, Control, and Defeat OCD (The ABCDs) are briefly reviewed, including the model for understanding OCD, the concept of habituation, techniques for doing Exposure and Response Prevention, and the techniques for changing fearful thinking. Finally, strategies for regaining gains after setbacks and managing stress are outlined. Deliver the message to your client that enjoying life is the best buffer against OCD!

References

Abramowitz, J.S., Whiteside, S.P., and Deacon, B.J. (2005). The effectiveness of treatment for pediatric obsessive-compulsive disorder: A meta-analysis. *Behavior Therapy, 36*, 55-63.

Franklin, M.E., Sapyta, J., Freeman, J.B., Khanna, M., Compton, S. Almirall, D., et al.(2011). Cognitive behavior therapy augmentation of pharmacotherapy in pediatric obsessive-compulsive disorder: The pediatric OCD treatment study II (POTSII) randomized control trial. *Journal of the American Medical Association, 306* (11), 1224–1232.

Freeman, J., Sapyta, J., Garcia, A., Compton, S., Khanna, M., Flessner, C., et al.(2014). Family-based treatment of early childhood obsessive-compulsive disorder: The pediatric obsessive-compulsive disorder treatment study for young children (POTS Jr) – A randomized clinical trial. *JAMA Psychiatry, 71*(6), 689–698.

Geller, D.A. & March, J. (2012). Practice parameter for the assessment and treatment of children and adolescents with obsessive-compulsive disorder. *Journal of the American Academy of Child and Adolescent Psychiatry, 51*(1), 98–113.

Scahill, H., Riddle, M.A., McSwiggan-Hardin, M.T., Ort, S.I., King, R.A., Goodman, W.K. (1997). Children's Yale Brown obsessive compulsive scale: Reliability and validity. *Journal of the American Academy of Child and Adolescent Psychiatry, 36*, 844–852.

Storch, E.A., Lehmkuhl, H.D., Rickets, E., Geffken, G., Marien, W., Murphy, T.K. (2010). An open trial of intensive family based cognitive-behavior therapy in youth with obsessive-compulsive disorder who are partial responders or nonresponders. *Journal of Clinical Child Adolescent Psychology, 39*, 260-268.

Torp, N.C., Dahl, K., Skarphedinsson, G., Thomsen, P.H., Valderhaug, R., Weidle,B., et al. (2015). Effectiveness of cognitive behavior treatment for pediatric obsessive-compulsive disorder: Acute outcomes from the Nordic long-term OCD treatment study (NordLots). *Behavior Research and Therapy, 64*, 15– 23.

Chapter 1

Diagnosis and Psychoeducation

Diagnosis and Psychoeducation

Finding your way in the world as a teen or almost teen is a big challenge. The questions you have as an adolescent are challenging and tough to answer: *How am I doing? What is life about? How do I fit in? Am I likable? Why do I feel so sad sometimes? What am I good at? What are my weaknesses? Why do other people seem to "get it" when I don't? Why don't my parents get it? What is the purpose of life? What does it mean to die? What's the right or wrong thing to do? Is there someone for me? Will I be successful? Will my friends continue to like me? Why do I feel so alone? How will my life turn out? Will I be happy?* All of us have dealt with these types of questions.

On top of grappling with these questions, if you have obsessive-compulsive disorder (OCD) you are also faced with the difficult task of learning how to control obsessions and compulsions. This book will help you understand OCD and get it under control. It provides information about **Actions** that can help you **Beat**, **Control**, and **Defeat** OCD. Consider this book the **ABCD** model for fighting OCD!

Types of OCD

OCD is a disorder that can have many different symptoms. See if you recognize yourself in these examples:

- Aaron washes his hands so many times that he can spend more than 20 minutes at the sink and over an hour in the shower.

- Brooke repeatedly checks her homework and to-do lists to make sure she has completed her assignments. She goes to bed very, very late as a result.

- Calvin worries that he didn't say his prayers correctly, so he says them over and over until he gets them right.

- Denelle counts her steps when she walks and then adds some steps so that she ends up on what she thinks is a good number.

- Ernesto repeatedly checks inside his closet and under his bed before going to sleep to make sure nothing will harm him.

- Fiona avoids petting her dog because she thinks she could get sick from the chemicals in the flea and tick medicine.

- Gemal avoids going near some of his classmates at school because he thinks that their bad luck will rub off on him.

- Hayley asks her parents over and over again to repeat what they said in order to be sure she heard their words correctly.

- Isaac says the phrase "Good, better, best" and counts to 10 when he has a thought that something bad might happen.

- Jenay takes hours doing her homework because she erases her writing repeatedly until she thinks it is perfect.

- Kody spends hours arranging and organizing all the things in his room. He constantly checks to be sure nothing is out of place.

- Laney says, "Good night, I love you," three times to her parents to be sure they won't die during the night.

- Malcolm avoids eating at school because he is afraid of being poisoned. At home he avoids eating any food that has been touched by anyone except himself.

- Nancy's fear that she might be attracted to other girls makes her avoid watching TV shows with cute girls in them. She also turns down invitations for sleepovers at her girlfriends' homes.

- Oberto picks up all the objects and scraps of paper he sees on the ground and saves them in boxes and bags that he keeps in his room.

- Paige cannot complete her book report because she has to reread every sentence in the book several times to make sure she understands it.

- Quentin avoids being around his good friends because he is afraid he will say something that will cause them to reject him.

- Rashida says "I'm sorry" to her parents nearly a hundred times a day because she is afraid she did something wrong.

- Stanley avoids being around children because he is afraid that he might touch them inappropriately.

- Tammy gets to school late every day because it takes her a long time to get cleaned up and dressed to her standard of perfection.

- Upton constantly counts everything he sees to a count of four. He spends so much time counting during the day that he's too tired after school to do anything fun.

- Vanessa has to sit down and get back up, go in and out of doorways, and look at things a certain number of times until it feels right.

- Will has to call up his mother many times throughout the day to make sure that she is all right.

- Xena avoids brushing her teeth and washing her hair because she is afraid that something very bad could happen that would change her life.

- Yanni has to say special phrases and count a certain number of times when he sees or hears words that he thinks would be offensive to God.

- Zoey changes her clothes many times during the day to avoid feeling contaminated.

You can see from these examples that there are many different types of OCD. They go from A to Z and beyond! Most of you will recognize yourself in more than one of the examples. It is common to have more than one type—you may have worries about touching certain things or people, you may wash your hands a lot, you may collect things, you may repeatedly ask questions, you may avoid certain people or places, or you may redo your actions until they feel right. Any combination of OCD symptoms is possible. The 26 examples you just read don't even include everything. The good news is that this book can help you with any type of OCD. **Actions** to **Beat**, **Control**, and **Defeat** OCD (a.k.a. the ABCDs of OCD) can be used for all the different types of OCD. You can learn how to **beat** OCD by reading this book.

What Is OCD?

Obsessive-compulsive disorder is an anxiety (*fear*) disorder that causes people to have ideas or images (*obsessions*) that make them afraid or uncomfortable. They take some action—say something or do something—to stop the thought and the worried feeling (the *compulsion*). Let's look back at the listed examples of children with OCD.

Remember Aaron? He washes his hands so many times that he spends 20 minutes at the sink and more than an hour in the shower. Aaron's unwanted idea or **obsession** is that touching things such as doorknobs and toilets can give him germs and make him sick. He washes to stop from getting sick. Washing is his **compulsion**.

Brooke checks and rechecks her to-do list many times to make sure she has completed her homework. She is worried that she won't get an A and that she will be a failure. Her worry about a bad grade and being a failure is the **obsession**, and checking repeatedly is the **compulsion**.

Hayley asks her parents over and over to repeat what they said because she wants to be certain that she understands *exactly* what they did say. Worry that she may be wrong is the **obsession**, asking them to repeat what they said is the **compulsion.**

Then there's Gemal. He avoids going near some of his classmates at school because he thinks that their bad luck will rub off on him. His idea that he can catch bad luck from some of his classmates is the **obsession**. Staying away or avoiding some of the kids at school is the **compulsion**.

Isaac says to himself "Good, better, best," and counts to 10 when he has a thought that something bad could happen. The fear that something terrible will happen is the **obsession**, what he says to himself is the **compulsion**.

Nancy's worries that she is attracted to other girls cause her to avoid watching TV and spending time with her girlfriends. The worry that she likes girls is the **obsession**, and avoiding her friends (and television) is the **compulsion**.

OCD Is a Worry Disorder

These examples show you what an **obsession** is: *an unwanted thought, worry, or image that makes you feel afraid, upset, or uncomfortable.* A **compulsion** is: *what you do or think to make the obsession go away.* That's how OCD works.

Your body makes chemicals in the brain – one is called serotonin. When chemicals like serotonin are out of balance, the signals in your brain are not sent correctly. This causes OCD. The OCD stops or drowns out the signals so that you end up worried when there is no reason to be – it is a false alarm. The OCD makes you do unneeded compulsions to shut the alarm off and stop the worry.

OCD is really a sly Trickster! It tries to make you believe things that aren't true. These are called obsessions or *imagined worries*. Then the OCD makes you do something to fix a worry that is not real.

The OCD Trickster is a *fake-out artist*! This book will help you see the difference between a *real worry* and an *OCD worry*. You won't be fooled by the OCD for much longer!

Normal Worries Are Different Than OCD Worries

So what is the difference between real, normal worries and fake OCD worries? Take Oberto as an example. He thinks that he has to pick up objects off the ground and save them. He is being tricked by the OCD. When is it important to pick up and save objects? When is it a good idea to leave things where they are? Is picking up all kinds of stuff off the ground something he needs to do? Is this a realistic worry? It certainly is not.

How do you know when something is a normal worry? Here are some things realistic situations that are normal to worry about:

- It is normal to worry about doing your best in school, but if you erase and re-erase to make your writing perfect, that is excessive and unnecessary.

- It is normal to save some sentimental things such as photographs, programs from plays, greeting cards, and letters. It is not normal to save candy wrappers, empty cartons, used bottle caps, or torn and used scraps of paper.

- It is normal to worry about getting sick. It is not normal to avoid touching doorknobs or using public restrooms.

OCD and Superstitions

Some OCD worries are like *superstitions*. Superstitions are excessive beliefs in luck, unrealistic beliefs, or ideas from long ago. Examples of some old-fashioned superstitions are fear of the number 13, avoiding bad luck by not walking under a ladder, or believing that breaking a mirror will bring seven years of bad luck.

So what is the difference between OCD and superstitions? They are alike in that superstitious behavior and compulsive actions are not realistic—or based on science. OCD compulsions are not based on science and fact. You can't prevent bad luck by avoiding friends or by saying phrases or counting. Nor can saying words, phrases, or counting cause good luck to happen. Try it. It doesn't work.

OCD also takes up more time out of a day than superstitions. OCD causes much more worry and fear than superstitions. OCD causes so much discomfort that it might make you stop doing everything until you can complete the compulsion. Superstitions, like avoiding walking under a ladder, seem silly when compared to OCD. But when superstitions turn into obsessions, like fear of the number 13, they can cause too much worry and fear.

If You Think You Have OCD

If you think you have OCD the good news is that there is help. Many kids, teens, and adults have OCD—and they have gotten help for it. In a school of 500 students, it is likely that at least a dozen kids have OCD. You are certainly not alone!

Talking about your OCD with your parents, teacher, guidance counselor, or school psychologist is a good thing to do, so that everyone can work together to get you the help you need.

There are two important kinds of help for OCD: *medicine* and *behavior therapy*. Many people with OCD take medicine that is given to them by psychiatrists. This medicine helps to balance the chemicals like serotonin in their brain so that the OCD worries and fears are lessened. Behavior therapy—what you will learn about in this book—is done by therapists such as psychologists and social workers who have special training in treating OCD. You can use this book to help you work with your therapist to tackle the OCD—to learn and to use the **actions** to **beat**, **control**, and **defeat** OCD (the ABCD's).

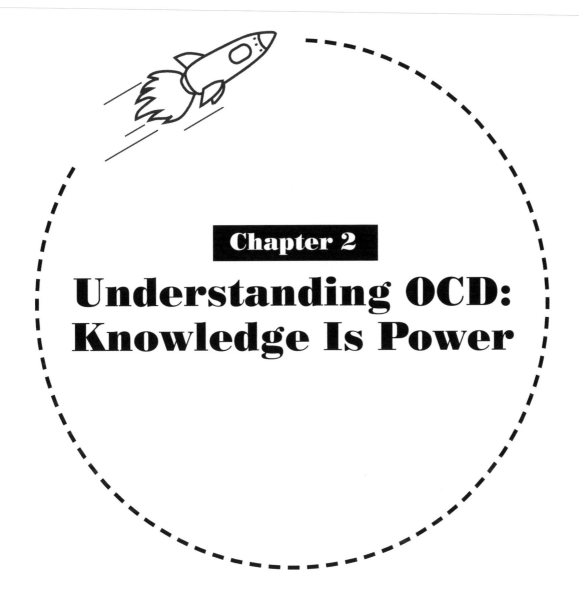

Chapter 2

Understanding OCD: Knowledge Is Power

Understanding OCD: Knowledge Is Power

The first **action** you need to **beat**, **control**, and **defeat** OCD is to understand it. Here are five things you need to know:

- OCD is a Trickster and a fake-out artist that tries to make you believe things that aren't true and make you do things you don't need to do.

- When you do what the OCD Trickster tells you, it makes the OCD stronger. It's like a bully pushing you around to get what it wants.

- When you don't listen to the OCD Trickster, you get stronger and the OCD Trickster gets weaker.

- You need courage to fight OCD. Tell yourself you can do it.

- By fighting OCD, you heal the chemical imbalance in your brain and you take back your own mind.

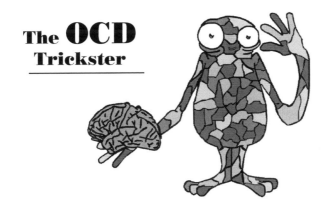

The **OCD** Trickster

How OCD Works

OCD works by grabbing hold of your brain and faking you out. The OCD Trickster makes you so afraid that you'll do almost anything it wants you to do. When you do what it tells you to do, the Trickster will make you do it again and again. This is called a *vicious circle*. You can see the *vicious circle* process in the picture on the next page.

Let's look at one example: The OCD Trickster puts the idea in your head that you must pick up a stick. The idea of picking up the stick is the **obsession**. Actually picking up the stick is the **compulsion**. Your worry and fear go away when you pick up the stick, and you feel better. The OCD Trickster is happy now that you did what it wanted you to do. It feels more powerful. And now that it is bigger and stronger it will make you pick up more sticks! The vicious circle has begun.

The more you give in to the OCD Trickster, the more it makes you do what it wants you to do. But there is a way out.

How OCD Vicious Circle Works

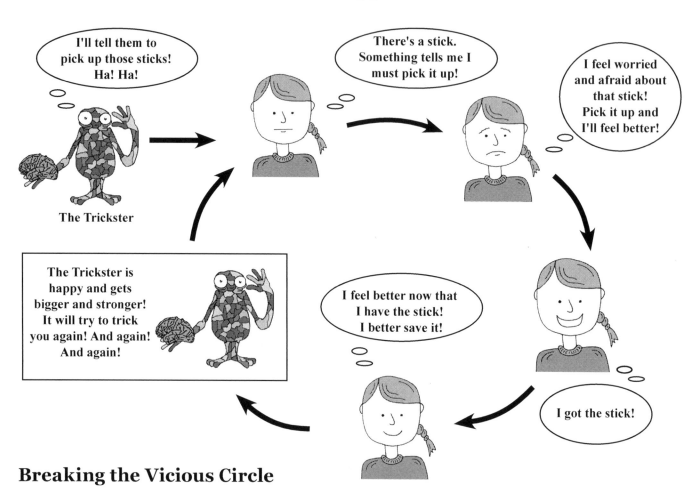

Breaking the Vicious Circle

When you don't listen to the OCD Trickster, you get stronger and the OCD Trickster gets weaker. Sounds easy but it can be a hard thing to do. The OCD Trickster is like a bully. And you know what happens when you give in to bullies. They bully you more. But bullies are really weaklings. They fake you out into thinking they are strong. They pick on people who they think are weak and who won't stand up to them. But when you do stand up to bullies, you learn how weak *they* are. I've done it myself even though I was scared. This is just what you need to do with the OCD Trickster.

Standing up to the OCD Trickster is the way to **beat** it, **control** it, and **defeat** it! You can see in the picture on the next page that this is the way to break out of the vicious circle.

Whatever the OCD tells you to do, you must try your best *not* to do it. When you stand up to the OCD Trickster, even though it is hard to do, you will get stronger. And each time you stand up to it you'll get stronger and stronger, and the OCD Trickster will get weaker and weaker. This takes courage and hard work. But this is how you break out of the OCD vicious circle. You *can* learn to do this! You can be helped by using the ABCDs: **actions** to **beat**, **control**, and **defeat** OCD.

How To Beat, Control and Defeat OCD!

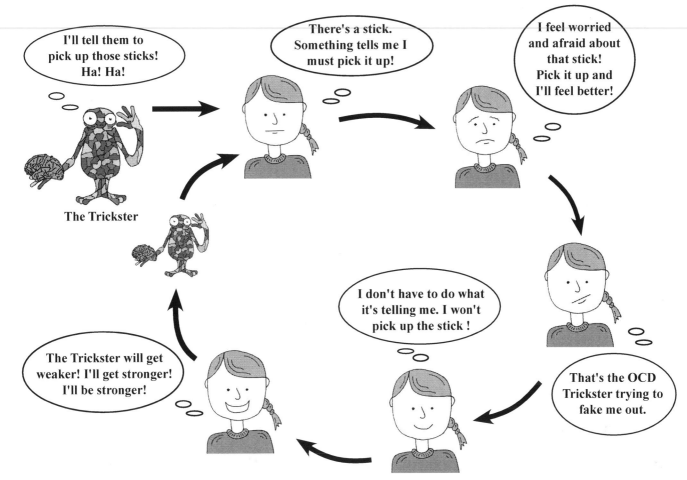

Behavior Therapy

Fighting OCD means learning not to give in to the OCD Trickster. Each time that you don't do what the OCD tells you to do, you take away the power of the OCD Trickster. This is what behavior therapy for OCD helps you to do. **Behavior therapy for OCD is called *exposure and response prevention*, or *ERP* for short.** It is the main action of all the ABCDs to beat OCD and it really works. This book will guide you all the way in learning how to beat back the OCD trickster.

Ernesto is a boy who has to check everything in his room several times before he can go to bed. He checks the lights to make sure they are turned off, he checks the windows to be sure they are closed, he checks the computer and the cell phone to be sure they are okay, and he checks the curtains, the closet, the door, and underneath the bed. He checks *everything*, and then he checks everything again, and again, and *again*, until he feels *right*.

The picture on the next page shows that Ernesto is caught in the OCD vicious circle. The OCD Trickster makes him feel that he has to check everything repeatedly. He goes to bed late because of what the OCD Trickster tells him. He feels so tired the next day that he falls asleep in school. It's really exhausting and frustrating for Ernesto. He can't seem to break out of the OCD vicious cycle.

What Happens When You Don't Give In to OCD

The OCD Trickster fakes out Ernesto so that he believes the only way to get rid of the fear and discomfort is to give in to what it says. The OCD Trickster is a liar! What Ernesto has to learn is that the uncomfortable feelings won't last. They may hang around for a while but if he waits them out and hangs in there, the worry and fear will go away. By pushing through the discomfort, he can **beat**, **control**, and **defeat** the OCD. This is what exposure and response prevention is all about.

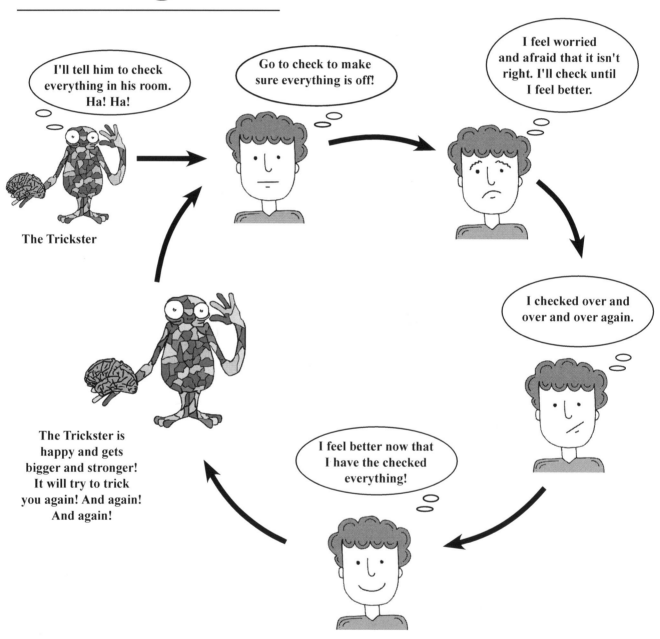

Ernesto's Checking Circle

The OCD Fear Rocket

When the obsession about checking starts up, Ernesto gets very afraid. It's as if he's stepped into a rocket against his will and then is suddenly blasted high into the sky, his fear and worry rising the higher the rocket gets. I call this the **Fear Rocket**. The ride on the Fear Rocket is so scary that Ernesto will do anything to get back to Earth. Doing the compulsion is the only way Ernesto believes he can get quick relief. In this case, pushing the button to get out of the rocket is the compulsion. His fear may be over in the short term, but he traded a safe and controlled landing away from the OCD for a quick exit. You can see in the picture that Ernesto falls quickly back down to Earth. By just riding in the rocket, he would have come in for a safe and controlled landing!

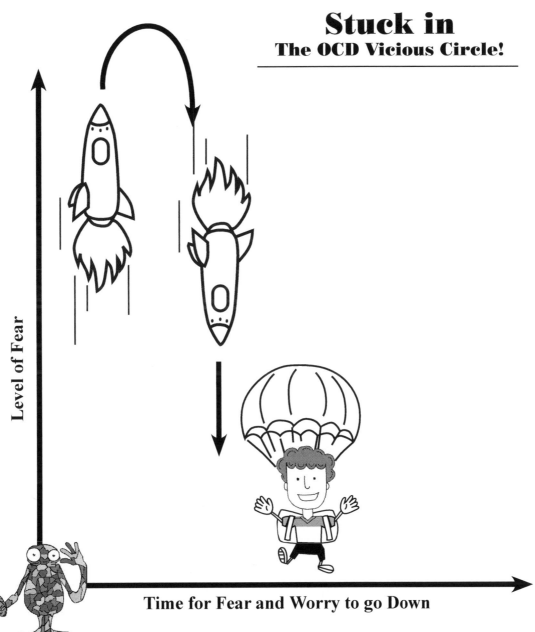

Stuck in The OCD Vicious Circle!

Level of Fear

Time for Fear and Worry to go Down

Breaking Free of OCD

The good news is that there is an **action** that Ernesto can learn to control the OCD: Bring his fear back down *without* doing the compulsion. He can *stay* in the Fear Rocket and ride in it slowly and safely back down to the ground! This means that the fear and worry he feels while he rides the OCD Fear Rocket will ease *without* doing the compulsion. Instead of getting out of the rocket, he can *take charge* of his fear by flying in the Fear Rocket safely down and away from the OCD.

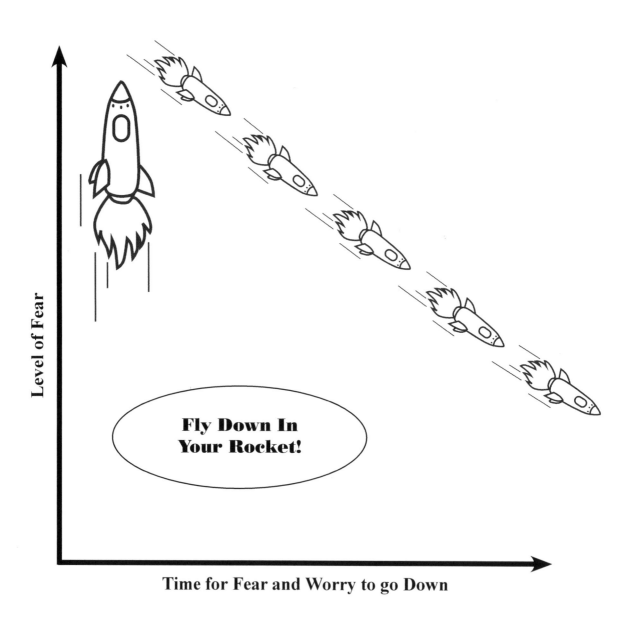

Level of Fear

**Fly Down In
Your Rocket!**

Time for Fear and Worry to go Down

Every time Ernesto stays in the Fear Rocket, he gets better and better at flying away from the OCD. It's like taking away the fuel from the rocket. The next time the Fear Rocket takes off it won't fly as high. Ernesto will be able to come back down to Earth quicker and quicker. Flying in the Fear Rocket by not doing a compulsion is what you need to do to **beat**, **control**, and **defeat** OCD.

Ernesto breaks out of the checking vicious circle by flying the Fear Rocket back down to Earth! This is tough to do, but he's much happier now that he doesn't have to do endless hours of checking at night. You can see this in the picture on the next page. Ernesto has stopped listening to what the OCD Trickster tells him to do. He becomes stronger than the OCD Trickster. You can learn that the Fear Rocket will steer back to Earth and you will break free from OCD.

Ernesto Breaks
The Checking Circle

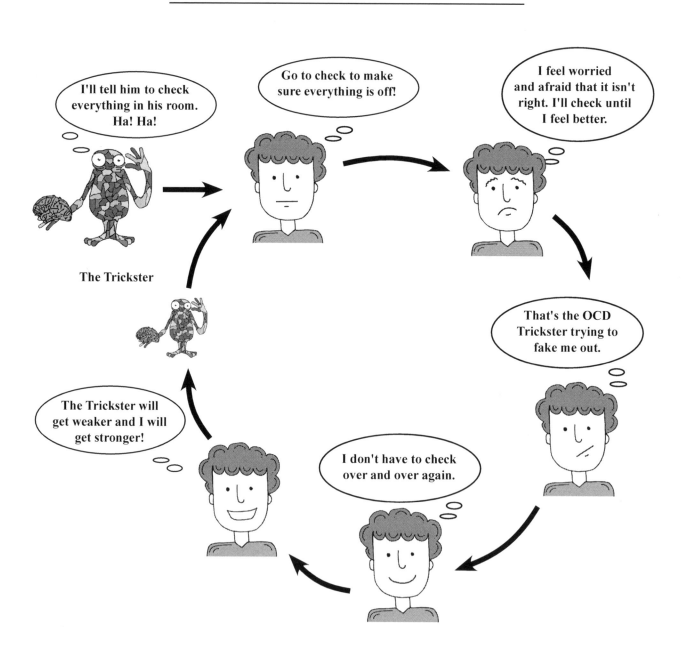

Understanding OCD

The picture below shows how OCD works. The OCD Trickster is very clever in getting you to worry about things that are not necessary to worry about. You break the vicious circle by not obeying the OCD Trickster. Understanding this is the start to breaking out of the vicious circle and **beating** the OCD!

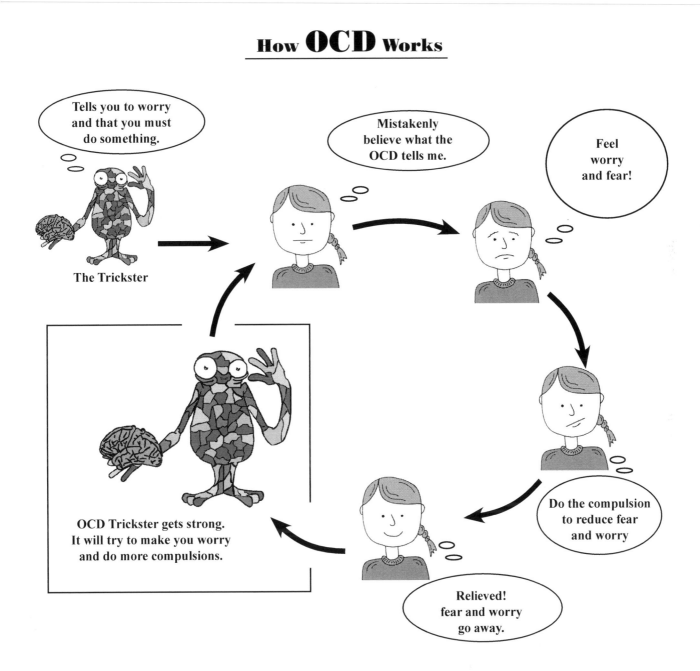

On the next page, you can see what you can do to **beat**, **control**, and **defeat** OCD.

How To Beat, Control and Defeat OCD!

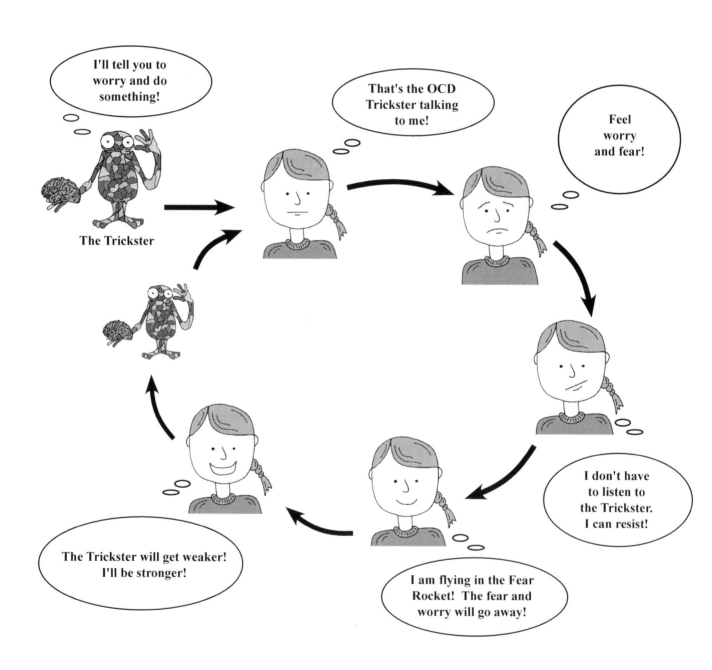

Worksheet

How to Beat, Control, and Defeat OCD

Use this form to practice the ABCDs of OCD.

1. Write down what the OCD Trickster tells you to worry about.
2. Tell yourself that you know it's the Trickster talking to you trying to scare you.
3. Tell yourself that there is no real reason to be afraid.
4. Tell yourself that you don't have to listen to the Trickster.
5. Tell yourself that you can ride the Fear Rocket safely back down to the ground.
6. Tell yourself that you are getting stronger and the Trickster is getting weaker.

19

How to Beat, Control, and Defeat OCD

Use this form to practice the ABCDs of OCD.

1. Write down what the OCD Trickster tells you to worry about.
2. Tell yourself that you know it's the Trickster talking to you trying to scare you.
3. Tell yourself that there is no real reason to be afraid.
4. Tell yourself that you don't have to listen to the Trickster.
5. Tell yourself that you can ride the Fear Rocket safely back down to the ground.
6. Tell yourself that you are getting stronger and the Trickster is getting weaker.

Getting Started: Standing Up to The OCD Trickster

Exposure and Response Prevention (ERP) means riding in the Fear Rocket instead of jumping out of it by doing the compulsion. Easy to say, but it can be hard to do. You have to be brave to fly in the rocket through clouds of fear and worry to a safe landing. Tell yourself that you can do it. Tell yourself that you are stronger, braver, and better than the OCD Trickster.

Tell yourself that you *can* succeed in beating the OCD. Tell yourself this every time you don't do a compulsion. Tell yourself this every time you don't avoid something scary. Assure yourself that every time you disobey the OCD Trickster you are getting stronger. Remind yourself of this every day. Tell yourself that you *can do this*!

To help get you going to **beat** OCD, think about the reasons for (pros) and reasons against (cons) fighting the OCD Trickster. Here are some examples that Ernesto gave:

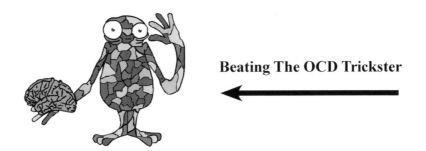

Beating The OCD Trickster

Ernesto's Pros and Cons

Cons for Beating the OCD Trickster	Pros for Beating the OCD Trickster
I will increase my anxiety trying.	I will feel good that I am trying to get better.
I will worry that my fears will come true.	I will have time to do what I like to do.
I will worry that I'll fail.	I will feel less embarrassed.
It will be hard work.	I will be healing my brain!

Now decide whether the pros or the cons are more important.

Cons

Think about each of the cons on the list:

- **I will increase my anxiety trying.** This may be true, but remember that the growing anxiety you feel when you *don't* do a compulsion is *temporary*. The more that you *don't give in* to the OCD Trickster, the lower the Fear Rocket goes up—and the faster you can fly it down for a safe landing. This book will teach you to build confidence in your ability to fly the Fear Rocket. The ERP **actions** you will learn will help you to cope with feelings of fear and worry—and lower your anxiety.

- **I will worry that my fears will come true.** The worry that what you fear (the obsession) will come true if you don't do the compulsion is exactly what the OCD Trickster wants you to think. The Trickster is faking you out! In these pages you will learn **actions** to test the truth of your fears. This will help you not to needlessly worry about the future. For example, Gemal thinks that if he goes near some of his classmates, some of their bad luck will rub off on him. By avoiding his classmates he is doing what the OCD Trickster tells him to do. Gemal is stuck in the OCD vicious circle. He needs to take a risk and stop avoiding his classmates. There is no such thing as perfect safety. Bad luck can happen to him whether he does or does not come in contact with his classmates.

- **I will worry that I'll fail.** This is the OCD Trickster trying to keep you from doing behavior therapy. Don't listen! In this book you will start with small steps that you can handle. You fly in the Fear Rocket first from lower heights of fear, and that makes it easier for you to *succeed*.

- **It will be hard work.** It may take a lot of effort to beat the OCD Trickster, but a little work every day will add up.

Pros

Now think about the pros. What are the advantages of fighting and **beating** the OCD Trickster?

- **I will feel good that I am trying to get better.** Feeling better is the goal of behavior therapy. Taking **action** to **beat** OCD can start to make you feel better. Reading this book and starting to fight the OCD Trickster can make you feel *great*.

- **I will have time to do what I like to do.** Compulsions are time-consuming and tiring. Think how wonderful it will be to do other activities, or even to just relax and do nothing at all!

- **I will feel less embarrassed.** Worry about hiding OCD from others is a drag. Freedom from fear of embarrassment is a relief and uplift.

- **I will be healing my brain!** Beating the OCD Trickster means you will take back your brain!

> What are some of the pros and cons that you can think of?

Worksheet

Beating The OCD Trickster

Write down your pros and cons.

Cons for Beating the OCD Trickster	Pros for Beating the OCD Trickster

Once you have written out your pros and cons for **beating** the OCD Trickster, check out whether the pros are more important than the cons. If the pros are not coming out ahead, you have more work to do to get yourself going. Getting a parent, friend, or teacher to help you with the list of pros can be just what you need to get you ready to take the next step. The ABCDs you'll learn in this book can help you **defeat** OCD—but it'll be an easier next step if your list of pros outweighs the cons.

☑ Check and Review to See What You Have Learned So Far!

- OCD is a trickster who tries to get you to do compulsions to get rid of fear and worry.

- The more you give in to the OCD Trickster, the stronger it gets.

- Exposure and response prevention—learning not to do what the OCD Trickster tells you to do—is the main **action** to break free and **beat** OCD.

- When obsessions start, the OCD Fear Rocket makes fear and worry go up. When you do the compulsion, your fear falls quickly back down.

- By flying in the Fear Rocket without doing the compulsion, the fear and worry take longer to come down, but by doing this you steer safely away from OCD.

- The more you fly the Fear Rocket, the less and less time it takes for the fear and worry to go down, and the faster you achieve a safe and controlled landing.

Chapter 3

ABCDs to Beat OCD – Behavior Therapy

ABCDs to Beat
OCD – Behavior Therapy

Cognitive behavior therapy helps you to learn effective **actions** to **beat**, **control**, and **defeat** OCD. The main action to do this is called exposure and response prevention. This means learning not to give in to the OCD Trickster and resisting the urge to do a compulsion. Flying in the Fear Rocket through the clouds, without jumping out, is what will give you control over OCD. There are three **action** steps to get ready for doing ERP.

- Identify all of your obsessions and compulsions.

- Rate how afraid you would feel about not doing each of the OCD behaviors.
  Use a scale from 1 to 10, easiest to hardest.

- Write out the list of OCD behaviors from easiest to hardest.

Identifying Obsessions and Compulsions

The first step to taking on the OCD Trickster is to identify all of your obsessions and compulsions. What does the OCD Trickster tell you to do? What do you do to reduce the worry and fear?

There are two main ways that you can respond to the OCD Trickster telling you to do something:

1. **Compulsions:** doing or thinking something that makes the anxiety go down. These are called *physical* or *mental compulsions.*
   - Jenay, who erases her writing repeatedly until it is *perfect*, gives in to the OCD Trickster by doing the physical compulsion of erasing repeatedly.
   - Isaac, who counts and says the phrase "good, better, best" in his head to prevent something bad from happening, is using a mental compulsion to make the fear and worry go away.

2. **Avoidance:** staying away from the things or situations that make you afraid and worried is called *compulsive avoidance.*
   - Malcolm avoids eating at school because he is afraid the food might be poisoned. This is an example of compulsive avoidance.
   - Nancy avoids her girlfriends and watching certain television shows because she is afraid that she might be attracted to cute girls.

The OCD Trickster has many tricky ways to make you afraid and worried. This is why it can be hard to identify all the different OCD obsessions and behaviors that you do. To help make your list of obsessions and compulsions, which you'll do at the end of this chapter, it may be useful to read over the examples listed in Chapter 1, beginning with Aaron and ending with Zoey. If you recognize yourself in an example, that is an obsession and compulsion you should include on your list.

Chapters 6 to 11 each teach you about a different type of OCD behavior; you might want to skip ahead now for examples similar to your OCD symptoms, as you think about what to put on your list of obsessions and compulsions.

Need more examples? Here are some common obsessions and compulsions:

Types of Obsessions

Contamination Obsessions

- Worry about germs or dirt
- Worry that everyday things contain poison
- Worries about chemicals, detergents, cleaners
- Worry about someone's bad luck, unattractiveness, unpopularity
- Worry about animals or insects

Ordering and Arranging Obsessions

- Worry about things or actions being balanced
- Worry about things being neat
- Worry about exactness
- Worry about things being aligned
- Worry about placement of things

Collecting and Hoarding Obsessions

- Collecting and saving things, including useless objects
- Too much concern with losing things
- Picking up useless or worthless objects
- Not using new items
- Not throwing things away

Perfectionism Obsessions

- Worry about using the right words in writing or speaking
- Too much concern with making mistakes or errors
- Excessive concern with grades
- Overconcern with appearance and grooming
- Worry about remembering or knowing

Harming Obsessions

- Unrealistic worry about hurting someone
- Unrealistic worry about hurting yourself
- Overconcern about protecting others
- Worry about aggressive or sexual thoughts
- Too much concern with responsibility for others

Illness and Safety Obsessions

- Unrealistic worry that you'll get a disease
- Unrealistic worry that you have a disease
- Overconcern with safety of family
- Unrealistic worry about being attacked physically
- Worry about being too careless

Moral and Religious Obsessions

- Too much concern with pleasing God
- Too much concern with praying perfectly
- Excessive worry about impure thoughts
- Doubting whether one is a good person
- Overconcern with punishment for being bad

Doubting Obsessions

- Worry that you don't remember something
- Worry that you didn't complete or do something
- Worry that you may have done something harmful
- Worry that you might be gay
- Worry that you did something embarrassing

Other Types of Obsessions

- Repeating songs, pictures, or ideas in your head
- Superstitions about good luck or bad luck
- Feeling right
- Clothes feeling right
- Looking in mirrors

Types of Compulsions

Cleaning and Washing Compulsions

- Washing hands too much or for a certain number of times
- Showering too much, too long, or for a certain number of times
- Changing clothes excessively
- Washing or wiping off belongings or possessions
- Avoiding touching or close contact with people or things

Checking Compulsions

- Repeated checking that lights, stoves, computers, and so on are off
- Repeated checking that doors, windows, shades, and so on are closed
- Repeated checking that family members are safe
- Repeated checking that you didn't do something bad or hurt anyone
- Repeated checking of homework

Repeating Compulsions

- Repeating actions until they feel right
- Going in and out of doors
- Repeatedly putting clothes on and off
- Repeating questions
- Rereading and rewriting

Counting Compulsions

- Counting objects in sets of specific numbers
- Counting actions such as steps or swallows
- Counting to reach a good number
- Touching or tapping objects a specific number of times
- Counting the number of words written on a line

Arranging Compulsions

- Arranging objects in a balanced way
- Organizing items in specific groups

- Arranging items in specific places

- Arranging items so they don't touch one another

- Arranging clothes to get dressed

Saving, Collecting, and Hoarding Compulsions

- Picking up useless or worthless items

- Keeping useless or worthless items that should be thrown away

- Not using new items or clothes

- Collecting so many objects that there is no room for them

Moral and Religious Compulsions

- Excessive praying

- Praying perfectly or until it feels right

- Apologizing or asking for forgiveness

- Confessing

- Not accepting good things or rewards

Avoidance Compulsions

- Avoiding people or situations

- Avoiding looking at or listening to certain shows or music

- Avoiding going to certain places

- Avoiding touching or coming in contact with specific numbers, words, pictures, and so on

- Avoiding talking about certain topics, people, situations, and so forth

Other Compulsions

- Reassurance seeking

- Thinking good thoughts to prevent bad thoughts or events

- Saying phrases, words, or numbers to prevent a bad event or to feel clean

- Staring at objects

- Doing things in a special way to avoid bad luck

Starting a Daily Diary of OCD Behaviors

Reading over these examples of some of the most common obsessions and compulsions can help you to identify your OCD behaviors. It may also be useful to keep a daily journal of your obsessions and compulsions, including both *what you do* and *what you avoid.* Pay attention to the situation or trigger that causes the obsession. This is the person, place, thing, image, or idea that sets off the OCD vicious circle. Writing things down for a few days can help you to pay attention and to keep better track of obsessions and compulsions. Record your observations as close to the time that they happen because you will remember them better that way.

To help identify her obsessions and compulsions, Sara, a girl with obsessions about counting, checking, and repeating actions until they feel right, paid attention to what she did and recorded them in her My Daily Diary. You can see Sara's diary for Monday on the next page. Sara also rated how afraid she would feel if she resisted doing each of the items in her list. To do this, Sara used the Fear Rocket Rating Chart on page 35. Sara assigned a number from 1 to 10 to each of her OCD behaviors. The numbers show how high the Fear Rocket would go if Sara resisted doing a compulsion. Sara then arranged her list from lowest to the highest. You can see Sara's list later in the chapter.

Sara's Daily Diary

Date & Time	Situation/ Trigger	Obsession: What the Trickster Tells Me to Do	Compulsion: What I Do	How I Would Feel If I Didn't Do The Compulsion – Fear Rocket Rating
Monday Dec. 7th				
10:30 am	Teacher explains homework. assignment.	Make sure you understand exactly what to do.	Repeatedly ask teacher to explain the assignment.	8
11:00 am	Sitting at desk at school.	Have to tap on legs.	Tap legs ending on a good number.	5
All Day	Using doors at home and school.	Go in and out until it feels right.	Go in and out repeatedly.	7
All Day	Swallowing.	Count swallows.	Count swallows to end on a good number.	6
All Day	Walking.	Count steps.	Count steps to end on a good number.	5
2:00 pm	Writing answer on test.	Write even number of words on each line.	Erase words if there is an uneven number.	9
4:30 pm	See sticks on the road.	Have to pick up sticks.	Pick up sticks.	4.5
6:00 pm	Doing math homework.	Avoid number 13.	Can't write 13.	2.5
6:30 pm	Writing worksheet.	Make sure words are written correctly.	Erase and rewrite words.	10
7:00 pm	Finishing homework.	Make sure all my homework is in my binders.	Check binders until it feels right.	10
8:00 pm	Reading.	Make sure you understand what you are reading.	Reread sentences.	10
9:00 pm	Going to bed.	Make sure the front door is locked.	Open and close the the lock 3 times	2

Worksheet

My Daily Diary

Fill out this diary every day.

Date & Time	Situation/ Trigger	Obsession: What the Trickster Tells Me to Do	Compulsion: What I Do	How I Would Feel If I Didn't Do The Compulsion – Fear Rocket Rating

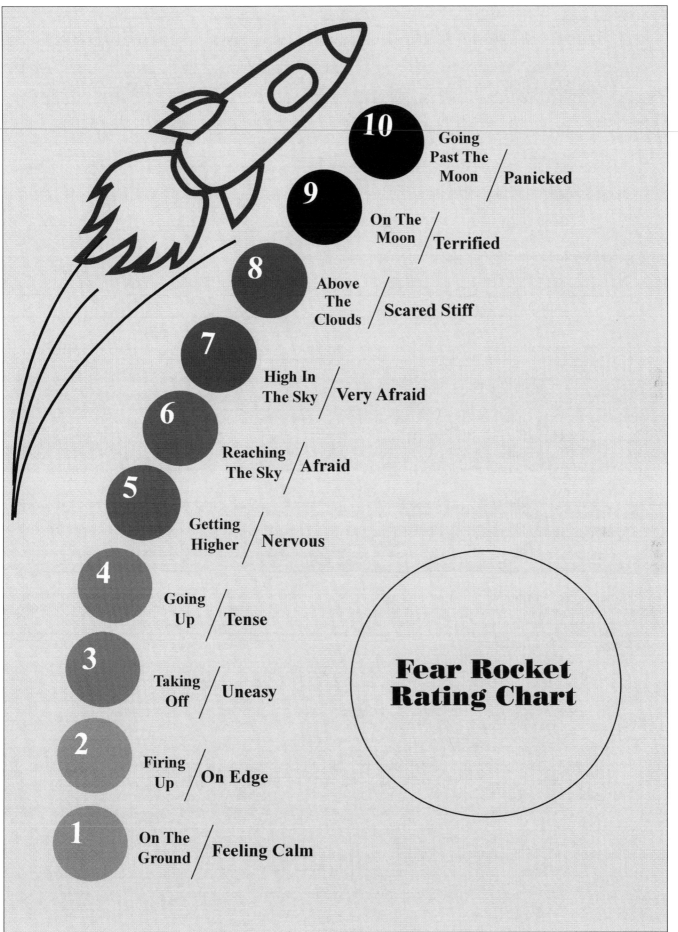

10 Going Past The Moon / Panicked

9 On The Moon / Terrified

8 Above The Clouds / Scared Stiff

7 High In The Sky / Very Afraid

6 Reaching The Sky / Afraid

5 Getting Higher / Nervous

4 Going Up / Tense

3 Taking Off / Uneasy

2 Firing Up / On Edge

1 On The Ground / Feeling Calm

Fear Rocket Rating Chart

Sara's List of Rated Obsessions and Compulsions

Obsessions and Compulsions	Fear Rocket Rating
Reduce erasing and rewriting words.	10
Check homework binders less.	10
Reread sentences twice instead of three times.	10
Write an uneven number of words on each line of writing.	9
Reduce the number of time I repeat asking questions to be sure that I understand.	8
Go in and out of doors one less time.	7
Count the number of times I swallow so that I end on a bad number.	6
End on a bad number when counting steps.	5
Tap legs ending on a bad number.	5
Don't pick up sticks.	4.5
Write the number 13 everyday.	2.5
Check the lock on the front door once instead of two times	2

Doing Exposure and Response Prevention (ERP)

ERP is done by trying to stop the compulsions. You start this by working on the compulsion that cause you the least fear. On Sara's list of obsessions and compulsions she gave a rating of 2 to the compulsion of checking the lock on the front door once instead of two times. This was an easy exposure for Sara. She practiced checking the door just once, each time rating how she felt according to the Fear Rocket. When Sara no longer feared checking the door once, she practiced not checking the door at all. She succeeded in doing this after a few times.

Sara then moved up to the next compulsion: writing the number 13 every day. With repeated practice and success on the easier items, Sara kept moving up the Fear Rocket to the compulsions more difficult to stop. For each step that she moved up the list, it took lots of practice, work, and determination. But the small steps added up.

By the time Sara gets to the compulsions that are the most difficult to stop, she will have more confidence about flying in the Fear Rocket because of her success in overcoming the easier compulsions. Sara will even be confident about staying in the Fear Rocket when it goes up very high—*past the moon*!

Sara's most difficult compulsion to stop was erasing and rewriting words. When she got to this compulsion, she practiced by writing just one word without erasing and rewriting. Then she practiced with two words, then three, then four, until she could write a whole sentence without erasing and rewriting. The first time she did this, Sara gave it a very high rating on the Fear Rocket. Each time her fear dropped down when she wrote a word, she practiced writing more words without erasing and rewriting. By taking *small steps* and *repeating the exposure many times*, the Fear Rocket didn't go up so high, and it took less and less time for Sara to fly to a safe landing.

Use the form on the next page to make your list of OCD obsessions and compulsions. Look back at your Daily Dairy to help you fill out this list. (If you haven't started the dairy, turn to page 34 to begin! This is a very important first step in the **actions** to **beat**, **control**, and **defeat** OCD!) Using the Fear Rocket scale on page 35 rate how scary it would be if you *did not* do each compulsion. Then reorder the list from lowest to the highest (or from easiest to hardest to accomplish) on the Fear Rocket. Your list of rated items will be your map, a starting point for doing exposure and response prevention. You can work on the list more as you go along learning more about the ABCDs.

My List of
Obsessions and Compulsions

List your obsessions and compulsions in the space provided and rate your fears.

Obsessions and Compulsions	Fear Rocket Rating Rating (1-10)

10 — Going Past The Moon / Panicked

9 — On The Moon / Terrified

8 — Above The Clouds / Scared Stiff

7 — High In The Sky / Very Afraid

6 — Reaching The Sky / Afraid

5 — Getting Higher / Nervous

4 — Going Up / Tense

3 — Taking Off / Uneasy

2 — Firing Up / On Edge

1 — On The Ground / Feeling Calm

Fear Rocket Rating Chart

How to Beat the OCD Trickster

The basic idea behind doing exposure and response prevention is that you have to be *brave*. You have to tell yourself not to give in to the OCD Trickster. You have to learn to steer your Fear Rocket! There are many useful **actions** that will help you to **beat**, **control**, and **defeat** OCD!

Following is a checklist of **actions** you have learned so far. Take the time to check off the ABCDs that you feel you have a strong handle on. For any topic that is missing a checkmark, read over those sections in this book for review. In the next chapter you will learn more about doing exposure response prevention.

Worioksheet

Actions to Beat, Control
and Defeat OCD Checklist

Actions	✓
Understand the OCD vicious cycle.	
Understand behavior therapy and ERP.	
Identify obsessions and compulsions.	
Rate and rank obsessions and compulsions.	
Understand the pros vs. cons of beating OCD.	
Tell yourself that you can beat the OCD Trickster.	
Understand that small steps lead to big gains.	

Chapter 4

ABCDs of
Coping with Fear

ABCDs of Coping with Fear

There are two main types of actions that can help you beat, control, and defeat OCD, no matter the type of OCD:

- Doing successful exposure and response prevention

- Understanding fear and how to manage it

Doing Successful Exposure and Response Prevention

When Sara tackled her list of obsessions and compulsions, she did exposure and response prevention exercises starting with the easiest items and moving up on her list in a step-by-step way to the hardest items. When you tackle your list of obsessions and compulsions, ERP is the main action to beat OCD. Here is a list of very good actions to help do ERP.

Fly the Fear Rocket to a Safe Landing

Each time you practice confronting the OCD Trickster by not doing a compulsion, it is important to ride the Fear Rocket *through* the clouds of fear and worry to a *safe* landing. By not giving in to the compulsion—not jumping out of the Fear Rocket—you will take power away from the OCD Trickster. You must stay in the rocket at all times. Remember: Ride the rocket through the clouds. You don't need to jump out, even when a situation feels scary.

Practice ERP Again and Again and Again

Practice is what makes us better at just about everything: math, sports, playing a musical instrument. It's also true with ERP. The more you practice ERP exercises, the better you get at controlling the OCD. The more times you fly the Fear Rocket, the better you'll get at landing safely. The Fear Rocket gets easier and easier to ride because it doesn't go up as high—and so it comes down faster—the more you practice. You get stronger and the Trickster gets weaker, and weaker, and weaker. It is the *repetition of the exposure practice that actually rebalances the chemistry of your brain.* So remember that exposure practice is the way to heal your brain.

Give Yourself Time

When you are in the Fear Rocket, it can feel like it is taking forever to come down to Earth. You will be tempted to give in to the compulsion and jump out. But you have to give yourself enough time for the fear and worry to lessen. It won't happen right away. As you do ERP, the time it takes for the fear and worry to go away will be shorter and shorter.

Break Down the Compulsion a Little at a Time

If it is too hard to stop the compulsion all at once, changing it a little at a time makes it easier. Sara did this with the compulsions about repeating questions, rereading, checking binders, and erasing and rewriting words. She practiced repeating questions less, rereading less, checking binders fewer times, and erasing and rewriting words less. When she succeeded in reducing the compulsion a little, then she reduced it again, and again, and again until she succeeded in stopping it completely.

Reward Yourself

Plan ways to reward yourself for doing ERP exercises. You can reward yourself immediately after you do an exposure exercise by planning some pleasurable event such as playing a favorite game, having an ice cream cone, watching a TV show, or whatever it is that you enjoy. You can also plan on working toward larger rewards by giving yourself points for exposure exercises—the points earned can vary according to the difficulty level of the exposures. Keep records of the daily exposures and the points earned. Decide on how many points it will take for you to reward yourself with something pleasant. Enlisting the help of a parent, family member, friend, therapist, or counselor in setting up a plan to work for rewards would also be useful.

Talk to Yourself

Remind yourself that you are practicing **actions** to **beat**, **control**, and **defeat** the OCD Trickster. Encourage yourself. Tell yourself that you are brave and that you can **beat** the OCD Trickster. Tell yourself that you can fly the Fear Rocket through the clouds of worry and fear to a safe landing. Say something like, "Every time I resist a compulsive urge, I am taking my brain back and making it better." Remind yourself that taking small steps will get you to the goal of **beating** the OCD Trickster.

Talk to the OCD Trickster

Talk to the OCD Trickster. Tell it that you know it's trying to fool you, that it's trying to put ideas in your head that are not true, that it is trying to steal your brain. Say, "You're a Trickster and I don't have to listen to you." Make up your own names for the Trickster like "The Faker," "The Fooler," "The Meanie," "The Liar," or "The Mind Thief." Call it by its name when you talk to it, and tell it that you don't have to listen to its silly orders!

Keep a Daily Diary

Pay attention to the situations when the OCD Trickster is likely to tell you to do a compulsion. Make a list of situations—places, persons, events, things, or thoughts—that trigger the obsessions. To do this it is useful to keep a Daily Diary (see page 34) for a few days to record your obsessions, compulsions, and what triggers them. This information can help you to be prepared and on guard for the Trickster in these situations.

Rehearse ERP Exercises

Practice exposure exercises *before* you get into trickster situations. This is like training for an athletic event or rehearsing for a live performance. Imagine ahead of time how you will do an ERP exercise. Write out in detail a situation where you are going to fight the OCD Trickster by not doing a compulsion. Read it over and then act it out. This is like preparing your muscles and your brain for action to beat the Trickster! Do this a few times.

Say the Fear—Get It Out of Your Head

Write down exactly what it is that you fear would happen if you *didn't* do the compulsion. For example, Sara is afraid that if she writes a word without erasing and rewriting, the word won't be written perfectly, she won't feel right, and she won't stop thinking about it until she can rewrite the word. Sara helped reduce her fears by writing down each fear repeatedly and saying them out loud repeatedly. She said, "The word I wrote is not perfect, I won't be able to stop thinking about it, and I won't feel right." Repeating this for 10, 15, or 20 minutes can make the Fear Rocket fly lower. When we confront a fear in this direct and repetitious way, the fear becomes less scary. This is a very powerful technique, but it can be tough to do, so you should practice this first with items that are low on the Fear Rocket scale. It may even be best to practice this technique with your therapist in order to get the hang of it.

Sing Your Obsession

Another way to get the fear out is to sing it. Sara could sing out her obsession to a familiar tune (for example, "The Farmer in the Dell"), or she could make up a tune of her own for singing out her fear. Singing is really a good technique to use when you are working on items that are high on the Fear Rocket. Singing can help you to see how you are being fooled by the OCD Trickster. And when you sing, put your whole heart and soul into your song. Singing out loud and strong can help you feel better!

Record Your Fear and Listen to It

Use a smartphone, computer, or other device to record your obsession either by saying it or singing it. Then play it back repeatedly to yourself. Do this for 10, 15, or 20 minutes at a time. The more you listen to it the better. This is another exposure exercise that will make the Fear Rocket fly lower and lower, so that you can fly in quicker to a safe landing.

Do the Opposite of the Compulsion

You can **beat** OCD by doing an **action** that is the opposite of the compulsion. In Sara's case, this would mean that she would deliberately write words in a sloppy way. This is a very powerful way to **beat** back the OCD Trickster. Other examples of doing the opposite from her list would be to deliberately count swallows, steps, and taps on her leg to end on a bad number. She could also intentionally write words so that they have an uneven instead of even number of strokes.

Exaggerate the Obsession

Making the obsession seem *even worse* than you think can help you **beat** back the OCD Trickster. This may seem strange at first, but it is a proven **action** against OCD. When it is done the right way, it can help you to see how silly the obsession really is. It's like turning the obsession into a cartoon, something so unrealistic, it doesn't appear scary anymore.

For example, Sara could use this technique to work on the compulsion about picking up sticks off the ground. She obsesses that she needs to pick up the sticks. She can exaggerate the obsession by saying something like this: "I won't pick up the sticks, and there will be so many sticks on the ground that I will have a hard time walking down the sidewalk. The sticks will pile up so high that I will have a hard time even walking out of my house. There will be so many sticks that I won't be able to keep up with them. A wheelbarrow, a truck, even a whole fleet of trucks won't be big enough to hold all the sticks. I will be surrounded by mountains of sticks as high as the clouds. I will be on the news, on the radio, on television, and on the Internet as the person responsible for the stick problem. People will know about me all over the world because I didn't keep up with picking up the sticks. By making her obsession into a story such as this, Sara may be better able to see how ridiculous the obsession really is.

Distract Yourself

Do some activity to take your mind off your fear and worry. You can call a friend, play a game, sing, listen to music, watch TV, read a book or magazine, practice playing music, or get some exercise—ride your bicycle, take a walk, or play basketball, soccer, softball, baseball, gymnastics, ice hockey, cheerleading, skating, tennis, badminton—the list goes on. The whole point of distraction is to change what you focus on and become involved in an activity that can help to make the fear go away.

Delay or Postpone Compulsions

When you expose yourself to a scary situation, instead of doing the compulsion immediately, such as checking the door or erasing and rewriting, try to delay giving in to the compulsion for at least a short time—5 minutes? 10 minutes? 15 minutes? Half an hour? An hour? Choose a length of time that you can succeed with while waiting out a compulsion. While you are waiting, do something else—exercise, text, go on the computer, play a game—anything that helps you to not do the compulsion.

Make an Appointment with the Obsession

When you feel an urge to do a compulsion, you can try to resist by scheduling a time later in the day, or even the next day, to do the compulsion. In Sara's case, when she has the urge to repeat asking questions, she could make an appointment with her parents to ask them questions the following day at 4 p.m. By the time 4 p.m. comes around the next day, she may have ridden in the Fear Rocket to a safe landing and the compulsive urge to ask questions may not be so strong. On the other hand, if she still wants to ask questions, she has the opportunity to do so at the scheduled time.

Set a Time Limit on Compulsions

You can beat the OCD Trickster by setting a time limit on how long you will do a compulsion. Sara might set a limit of 5 minutes for asking and re-asking questions. This limit-setting technique gives you practice resisting doing compulsions while also providing an outlet for the urges. Eliminating the compulsions altogether is still the main goal.

Practice Not Avoiding

Avoiding scary situations so that you don't have to do a compulsion is another way to give in to the OCD Trickster. The more you avoid something because of fear the scarier the situation becomes. Stop avoiding as much as possible. Gemal is the boy who avoids going near some of his classmates because he fears that their bad luck will rub off on him. The more he avoids the situation, the stronger his fear becomes. Avoidance makes the OCD Trickster stronger. Less avoidance helps to beat the Trickster. You can start to avoid less by doing it a little at a time.

Think About Your Friends

Think about your friends who don't have obsessions and who don't do compulsions. They are in the same situations as you—and they're doing okay. Before you developed OCD you were like your friends. You can **beat** OCD and be like your friends again.

Get a Helper

Having someone to support you when you do ERP exercises can help you to beat the OCD Trickster. In addition to your therapist, a parent, a sibling, or even a friend can help you. Whoever it is, it is very important that he or she understand what you are trying to do when you try to resist doing compulsions. Your therapist can teach your helper what to do. Reading this book can help your helper learn about OCD, the Trickster, the ABCDs, and how to do exposure and response prevention. The helper can act like your coach, your trainer, and your cheerleader in encouraging you to fight and resist doing what the OCD Trickster tells you.

Find a Support Group

Attending a support group for OCD, especially one that is professionally led, can help you carry out your ABCDs. If there isn't a group near you, try joining an online community that is focused on behavior therapy for OCD.

Understanding Fear and How to Manage It

When you face off with the OCD Trickster by not doing a compulsion, the Fear Rocket blasts off into the sky. Your feelings of fear and worry can be very uncomfortable. It may seem very difficult not to jump out of the Fear Rocket by doing a compulsion.

You have just learned several **actions** you can do to take charge of the Fear Rocket and ride in it back to safe ground. But have you ever thought about what fear really is? Have you ever wondered why we feel fear in the first place? When you understand how fear works, you can take control of it.

Recognize Fear as Normal

Understanding that there is nothing dangerous about feeling scared or worried can help. Fear is a normal feeling. It is as normal as feeling happy, shy, embarrassed, tired, hungry, sad, and so on. Everyone you know has felt scared or worried at some point. All animals have the ability to feel fear. In fact, survival depends a great deal on fear—if our ancestors weren't afraid of saber-toothed cats, you might not be alive!

Understand the Fight-or-Flight Reaction

Fear is part of the fight-or-flight reaction. Nature gave us this alarm response to help us defend ourselves when faced with danger, like against all those prehistoric animals with sharp teeth. When this happens we experience bodily feelings, scary thoughts, and a strong urge to act by fighting or fleeing.

When you become afraid in the face of *real* danger, such as someone attacking you, the fight-or-flight reaction is very useful. It's like an alarm going off inside your body that springs you into action to deal with the scary threat. When you become afraid in the face of an *unreal* danger, such as those situations brought on by OCD, the fight-or-flight reaction is not useful. It's like a false alarm–you go into action for no reason. When this happens, you use up energy unnecessarily. You go up in the Fear Rocket—way, way up in the sky.

What is important to understand is that the feelings of fear caused by OCD are *not* caused by a real and true threat. The feelings of fear and worry are caused by an unreal or imaginary threat danger. So the good news is that you can learn to lessen your fear reaction and ride the Fear Rocket safely back down.

Fear has three parts: thoughts, feelings, and actions. The three parts of the fight-or-flight reaction have a protective purpose. When faced with danger, we have the thought or idea that something bad could happen (*thoughts*), our body gets pumped up (*feelings*), and we act by running or fighting (*actions*).

If you were swimming in the ocean and saw a shark fin pop up in the water, you would be alarmed and have a fight-or-flight reaction. Your heart would beat faster to send blood with oxygen into your muscles, you would breathe faster to get more oxygen, your muscles would tense up, and adrenaline would be released to give you the energy you need to get away or to fight. You would be able to swim as fast as you could away from the danger. Once you got safely away, you would feel tired because you used up all your energy in the emergency. Once you get rest and food, your body will be ready again to help you in an emergency.

Let's look at a chart on the below showing the three parts of the fight-or-flight reaction.

The Fight-or-Flight Reaction

Thoughts	Feelings & Physical Symptoms	Reactions
This is a dangerous situation. *Something bad could happen.* *I could be harmed. People could be hurt.* *Something terrible could happen.*	Increasing heart rate Tight chest Breathing harder Breathlessness Trouble swallowing Dizziness/light-headedness Blurry vision, spotted vision, or tunnel vision Tight muscles Trembling, shaking, quivering Numbness and tingling on skin Redness or flushing of the face Dry mouth Nausea or butterflies in stomach Cramping Diarrhea Tiredness or exhaustion	Escape (flight) Get angry (fight) Avoid the situation

As you can see from the chart, *avoidance* is another way to react when faced with fear. Compulsions are examples of avoidance. When the OCD Trickster gets you to believe an unreal threat, the fight-or-flight reaction kicks in, and you do a compulsion to escape from or avoid the fight-or-flight feelings. The key action to beating the OCD Trickster is to practice NOT doing a compulsion. You may experience some fight-or-flight feelings when you stop a compulsion. You may be uncomfortable for a while, but the fear symptoms *will* eventually go away. This is what happens when you ride the Fear Rocket to a safe landing instead of doing a compulsion.

So what can you do to cope and to calm yourself down when you are trying not to give in to a compulsion? Read on to find out.

Practice Deep Breathing

Using a deep, slow breathing technique can help you to manage anxiety. It helps to reduce the bodily feelings of fear and to clear your mind of the scary thoughts. Until you get the hang of it, do this exercise when you are not feeling any fears. Practice in a setting that feels safe and where you can lie down comfortably.

To begin, lie down and place one hand on your stomach just above your belly button and below your ribs. Put your other hand on your chest. Take a long, deep breath. When breathing in, let the air fill your lungs so deep that it lifts up your tummy. When you breathe out, do so gently and slowly, and feel your stomach go back down. Don't force your stomach in or out, let the air do it.

Once you feel comfortable feeling your breath go in and out, close your eyes and say "one" to yourself as you breathe in, then say "relax" to yourself as you breathe out. On the next breath say "two" as you breathe in, say "relax" to yourself as you breathe out. Do the same deep, slow breathing cycle up to a count of 10. This should take about one minute. Practice this for 5 minutes twice a day.

With practice you can do this without lying down. When you really learn it, you can use the deep, slow breathing anytime and anywhere to cope with fear. You can also use the deep breathing to help manage the fear you feel when you resist doing a compulsion. Do the deep, slow breathing for a few minutes until the fear goes down.

Try Picturing Pleasant Scenes (called Visualization)

Picturing a safe and relaxing scene is another way to cope with fear and worry. You can do the deep, slow breathing exercise while picturing a pleasant place like the beach on a summer day, a trail through a forest, a mountaintop meadow, or any place that you can think of that helps you to feel relaxed. When you think of your scene, imagine it in as much detail as you can, imagine all of the sights, the sounds, and the smells. Picture yourself in the scene and how you would feel. Here is an example:

Imagine yourself at the beach on a warm and beautiful summer day. Standing on the beach, you feel the warm sand under your feet, you feel the warmth of the sun on your body, you feel the warm sea breeze on your skin, and you hear the sound of the waves on the shore and the seagulls calling in the distance. The clouds are moving overhead, kites are waving in the wind, and sailboats are out on the water. It is a perfect day for you to relax. You are enjoying all the sights, sounds, and smells of the beach. As you breathe in you are refreshed by the smell and the feel of the salty sea air. As you breathe out your muscles relax and your mind calms. You can feel yourself feel more and more relaxed as you take in all the sights and sounds of this beautiful summer day. You take slow and easy breaths as you look out over the beach, the water, and the horizon. You feel more and more at ease. You feel calm, content, and relaxed.

My Relaxing Scene

Practice imagining a relaxing scene for yourself. Write your description below, including as much detail as possible.

Practice your deep-breathing exercise while imagining your relaxing scene. It is important to be patient with your practices. Just like the exposure exercises, the more you do deep breathing and visualizations, the better and better you will get with them. Then when you get anxious you can use them to help yourself calm down. The relaxation **actions** are good for everyone to use—after all, once you **beat**, **control**, and **defeat** OCD, there will be other situations in life that will make you feel worried and afraid. You can use your relaxation actions to help you in those situations as well.

Learn Progressive Muscle Relaxation

Another useful relaxation technique involves tensing and then relaxing the muscles in each part of your body. As with deep breathing and visualizations, until you get the hang of progressive muscle relaxation, do this exercise when you are not feeling worried, scared, or anxious. Practice in a setting that feels safe and where you can lie down comfortably.

Start by holding your arms straight out from your sides and make your hands into a fist. Squeeze your hands as tight as you can and contract all the muscles in your arms for 10 seconds. While tensing your arm and hand muscles, pay attention to how tense the muscles feel in your fingers, thumbs, wrist, forearm, and elbow. Now relax your hands and arms, letting them rest gently near your sides. Now pay attention to how your hands and arms feel while they are relaxed.

Repeat the exercise, focusing on the difference between the feelings of tension and feelings of relaxation in your muscles. Now hold your arms out straight from your shoulders with your palms facing the ceiling. Bend your arms at the elbow and tense your bicep muscles. Hold for 10 seconds, and then relax. Do it again and pay attention to the feelings of tension and relaxation.

Do the same tensing and relaxing with all your muscles. Doing each twice in a row: Tighten and pinch your shoulder blades together, then relax; squeeze and raise your shoulders up to your ears, then relax; stretch your legs out, contract your leg muscles, and point your toes, then relax; contract your legs muscles again but flex your feet this time, then relax; tighten your stomach, sit up as straight as possible, then relax back down; tighten your face muscles and squeeze your eyes shut, then relax.

After you have tightened and relaxed all the muscles, take 2 minutes to do your deep-breathing practice while imagining your relaxing scene. Focus on your feelings of relaxation at the end of the progressive muscle relaxation exercise.

The progressive muscle relaxation exercise helps you to feel calm. By practicing it every day for a week, you learn to pay attention to bodily signals about tension vs. relaxation. Once you have learned how to do progressive muscle relaxation, you can use a shorter version to help you calm down when you are out and about during the day: Simply tense and relax muscles in just one part of your body, such as your shoulders, squeezing them up to your ears for 10 seconds, then relaxing for 10 seconds, then repeating once more. You can do this anytime, anywhere to avoid compulsions.

Actions You Learned In this Chapter

Not everyone with OCD experiences the three parts of the fight-or-flight reaction when the OCD Trickster makes them afraid. Some people may experience the fear mostly as scary thoughts. The relaxation techniques of deep breathing, visualization, and progressive muscle relaxation may still be useful to help you manage your scary thoughts. Counting your breaths as you breathe in and out gets you to refocus your attention away from scary thoughts. Other techniques such as talking to yourself and talking back to the OCD Trickster can help you resist doing a compulsion. And by practicing the relaxation exercises you can certainly use them for fears and worries not related to OCD.

Next is a checklist of the **actions** you learned about in this chapter for doing exposure and response prevention. It may seem like there are many ERP techniques, but the first two are the main ones: Fly in the Fear Rocket to a safe landing and give yourself time.

Make several copies of this list and post it where you will see it often: On your bedroom door, in your school binder, or on your refrigerator. Or take a picture of it to keep on your smartphone. Then check off the ERP actions and exercises as you do them. And by all means, do them often!

As you learn more about the different types of OCD in the chapters ahead, you'll see how you can use other behavior therapy actions to help you do ERP.

Worseet

Exposure and Response Prevention Checklist

Place a check mark in the box when you have completed the exercise to land the fear rocket.

Exposure and Response Prevention Actions	✓
Fly in the Fear Rocket to a safe landing.	
Give yourself time.	
Practice ERP again and again and again.	
Break down the compulsion a little at a time.	
Reward yourself.	
Talk to yourself.	
Talk to the OCD Trickster.	
Watch Out for the Trickster.	
Rehearse ERP exercises.	
Say the fear—get it out of your head.	
Sing your obsession.	
Record your fear and listen to it.	
Do the opposite of the compulsion.	
Exaggerate the obsession.	
Distract yourself.	
Delay or postpone compulsions.	
Make an appointment with the obsession.	
Set a time limit on compulsions.	
Practice not avoiding.	
Think about your friends.	
Get a helper.	
Find a support group.	
Do relaxation exercises.	
Practice deep breathing.	
Try visualizations.	
Learn and practice progressive muscle relaxation.	

Chapter 5

ABCDs of
Fearful Thinking

ABCDs of
Fearful Thinking

How you *think* can make OCD worse or better. Changing how you think can help you to do behavior therapy. In this chapter you will learn about the following:

- Types of fearful thinking

- How to change fearful thinking

- Actions to think more realistically

Fearful Thinking

You have already learned that what you say to yourself can affect the OCD Trickster. If you tell yourself that you have to do what the Trickster tells you to do so that you will feel better, you are likely to do a compulsion. If you tell yourself that it is just the OCD Trickster trying to fool you, and that you don't have to do what it says, you are likely to beat back the Trickster. What you say to yourself matters!

There are ways of thinking that can make OCD better or worse. It is important to learn how to identify the thought patterns that make you give in to the Trickster. Once you learn about them, you can learn how to change them into thoughts that will help you to **beat**, **control**, and **defeat** the Trickster.

We have many, many thoughts in our head throughout the day, too many to count! From the time we wake up until the time we go to bed, we constantly talk to ourselves. Our mind is really a busy place. What we say to ourselves has a big impact on how we feel and what we do. *Our thoughts are the cause of our feelings and actions.*

Recall the example about seeing a shark fin near you in the water. You would certainly see it as dangerous and swim away. If it turned out that the fin was just an inflatable toy pushed by a friend trying to scare you, you might laugh or you might yell angrily at your friend for the prank. This example shows that how you interpret the situation can lead to very different reactions. The Trickster is like the fake shark fin in the water. Thinking that it's a joke and not really dangerous can help you face it and not run away.

Starting now, it is important to pay attention to what you say to yourself. Why? Because by changing your thoughts, you can change your feelings and your behavior. Seeing the Trickster for what it is, a fake-out artist, will help you be less afraid and **beat** it back!

In the next example Kody talks to himself about the situation of his room.

He says to himself that his room is a mess and that he won't feel right until it is organized. You can see that Kody's thoughts cause him to worry about his room and spend hours straightening and organizing the things in it. Kody is caught in the OCD straightening and organizing vicious circle! What he says to himself is keeping him stuck there. He can get free from the vicious circle by changing his thinking.

You can see in the following picture that what we say to ourselves can make us feel either good or bad. Your thoughts cause your feelings and your actions. I'll say that again - thoughts cause feelings! Change a thought and you'll change how you feel and what you do! Recognizing your thoughts, what you are saying to yourself, is the first step to change what you feel and what you do!

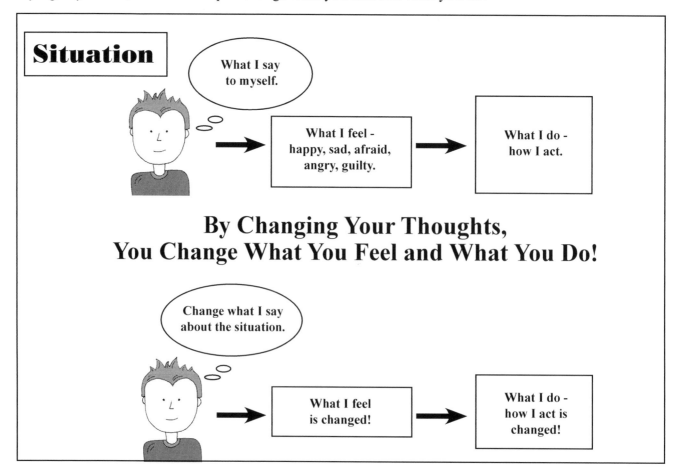

Kody has to recognize that the OCD Trickster is fooling him into believing that his room needs *a lot* of straightening and organizing. Kody has to ask himself if there is another way to look at his room situation. The fact that Kody can't get his homework done or have time for fun should show him that he is cleaning and straightening more than necessary. Changing how he thinks can help him to feel happier and to spend less time straightening and organizing. The next picture shows how Kody changed his thinking about his messy room. He feels better now and has time to do his homework. Changing his thinking helped Kody break out of the OCD vicious circle.

Understanding how to change your thinking starts with learning about how the Trickster makes you think about things incorrectly.

Types of Errors in Thinking

There are 10 common types of errors in thinking that help the OCD Trickster fool you into doing compulsions.

1. **Overestimating:** Exaggerating the likelihood that something bad will happen. You mistakenly predict or expect that something bad will happen.
    Examples:
    - Fiona believes that she could get sick from her dog's flea collar.
    - Will calls his mother at work repeatedly because he thinks something bad has happened to her.

2. **Over-responsibility:** Exaggerating your responsibility for bad things happening. Thinking that you are mostly or solely responsible for preventing something bad from happening, or that you are responsible for the bad event if it does occur.
    Examples:
    - Oberto picks up sticks so that no one will trip and fall.
    - Laney believes that if her parents are harmed in any way she is responsible.

3. **Catastrophizing:** Exaggerating the negative effects of something bad happening; making something out to be worse than it really is. This is the belief that if some negative event does occur, it would be terrible and you wouldn't be able to cope with it.

   Examples:
   - If Paige gets less than an A on a test, she thinks her life will be ruined.
   - If Kody's room is messy, he says he can't stand it.

4. **Filtering:** Exaggerating negative things and ignoring positive ones. This is the tendency to identify more negative than positive things. It's like the blinders on a horse that block the horse's view. You block yourself from seeing the positive things all around you.

   Examples:
   - Kody doesn't see that mostly everything in his room is in place.
   - Tammy can't see how nice she looks because she focuses on a wrinkle on her blouse or a hair out of place.

5. **Shoulds:** Exaggerating the importance of things. This means the tendency to think that things have to be done a very specific way, or only one way. It means holding on to a very rigid view of how something should or ought to be done.

   Examples:
   - Kody thinks that everything in his room should be neat and organized.
   - Calvin believes that prayers *should* be said with perfect concentration—if not, they don't count.

6. **Superstitious or magical thinking:** Exaggerating your influence and control. This is the tendency to believe that you can do something, or say something, to make something happen or not happen. This is done by saying certain words or phrases, avoiding certain words or phrases, performing some action, or avoiding doing a certain action.

   Examples:
   - Isaac says the phrase "good, better, best" to prevent something bad from happening.
   - Vanessa has to go in and out of doors a certain number of times in order to have good luck.

7. **Black-and-white thinking:** Exaggerating how good or bad something is. This is the tendency to see things as either completely positive or completely negative. This is called all-or-nothing thinking.

   Examples:
   - If one thing is out of place in Kody's room, then the room is a mess.
   - If one word is not written perfectly, then Jenay thinks that the whole page has to be rewritten.

8. **Fortune telling:** Exaggerating your ability to know what will happen. This is the belief that you can predict what will happen in the future.

   Examples:
   - Brooke thinks that she won't get into a good college if she gets a bad grade.
   - Upton believes that seeing certain numbers is a sign that something bad is going to happen.

9. **Mind reading:** Exaggerating your ability to know what people think. This is the belief that you can tell what others are thinking.

    Examples:
    - Hayley thinks that her parents will be disappointed in her if she doesn't understand exactly what they say.
    - Quentin thinks that his friends at school think he is weird.

10. **Thought-action-fusion (or confusion!):** Exaggerating how real a thought is. This is the tendency to believe that thinking a certain thought means that the thought is real, or that thinking just the thought of something can actually make it happen. It is a tendency to think that what is in your mind is factual or true when it is just something you have imagined. It exists only in your mind.

    Examples:
    - Nancy believes that if she thinks that a girl is cute then that means that she must be gay.
    - When Stanley thinks that he touched a child inappropriately, then he believes that he actually did do it.

Once you know about the errors in thinking, the next step is learning how to identify them in your own thinking.

Identify the Thinking Errors

You can start to identify the thinking errors in your own thoughts by paying attention to your negative feelings. When you feel upset, worried, afraid, angry, guilty, or sad, that is the time to pin down your thoughts. Ask yourself the following questions to find out what you are thinking.

- *What am I saying to myself?*

- *What is going through my head?*

- *What am I saying is going on here?*

- *What am I predicting is going to happen?*

- *What do I expect to happen?*

- *What do I think that they are thinking?*

Figuring out the answers to these questions can help you identify the thoughts that are causing the negative feelings. Knowing your thoughts can help to resist the OCD Trickster telling you to do a compulsion.

7 Steps to Change Thinking Errors

The goal of changing your thinking errors is to change your *exaggerated* thinking into *realistic* thinking. The Test Your Thought graphic that follows shows how this can be done. The first step to changing errors is to write down what you are saying to yourself. Go ahead and do that now in the space provided.

Step 1: My mistaken thought: _____

_____

_____

_____

Now rate how much you believe it on a scale from 0 to 100 percent.

Step 2: How much I believe this thought: _____ %

Next you can sort out how true the thought really is.

Step 3: How do I feel? _____

Test and Revise Your Thinking

Scientists figure out whether something is true by looking at evidence or facts. They test a prediction or hypothesis by looking at the facts or the evidence. They look at the facts that support the prediction as well as the facts that do not support it. Scientists are like detectives. Detectives examine evidence to find out what is true vs. what is false. When the evidence is false they revise their thinking. You can investigate your own thoughts just like a scientist studying facts or a detective investigating evidence.

Write down the facts that support what you are saying, as well as the facts that go against what you are saying.

Step 4: Facts that support my thought:

_____

_____

_____

_____

Facts that don't support my thought:

_____

_____

_____

After examining all the facts, ask yourself if your thought is supported by the facts: *Is it real?* Or is it not supported by the facts: *Is it an exaggerated idea that exists only in my own mind?* If it's an exaggeration, or just something in your imagination, you can change how much you believe it on the 0 to 100 percent scale.

Step 5: How much I believe the thought after reviewing all the facts: _____%

Come Up with Another Way of Looking at the Situation

Now that you have revised your thought based on facts, and you have revised how much you believe your thought, can you come up with another, more realistic way to look at the situation? Write down your new way of thinking about the situation.

Step 6: My revised thought about the situation: _____

_____

_____

Step 7: How do I feel now? _____

_____

_____

Looking at the situation in this more realistic way can change how you feel. This technique—examining your own thoughts by looking at evidence—and revising your thinking depending on what you find, is an important **action** that can help you beat OCD.

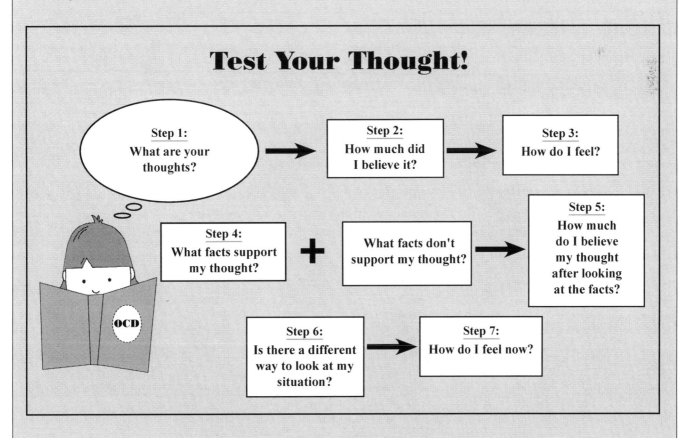

Test Your Thought!

Step 1: What are your thoughts?

Step 2: How much did I believe it?

Step 3: How do I feel?

Step 4: What facts support my thought?

+

What facts don't support my thought?

Step 5: How much do I believe my thought after looking at the facts?

Step 6: Is there a different way to look at my situation?

Step 7: How do I feel now?

OCD

The next diagram shows how Kody can test and revise his thinking about his room. Kody identifies his thoughts about his room, rates how much he believes that they are true, and examines whether the facts support or don't support what he is saying to himself. The diagram shows what Kody did to analyze mistakes in his thinking.

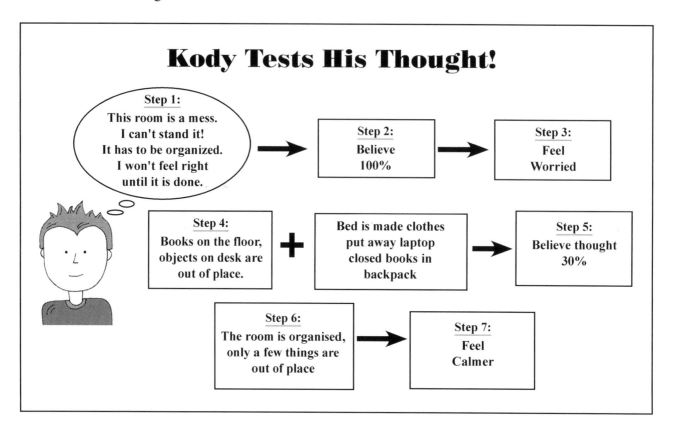

This room is a mess. This thought is not supported by the facts. Only a few things are out of place—most of the room is organized. This is an example of the *filtering* thinking error. Kody focused only on the things out of place.

I can't stand it. This thought is not supported by the facts because saying the room is a mess is an *exaggeration*. This is an example of the *catastrophizing* thinking error. Kody exaggerated his reaction to a few things out of place. He can cope with a few things being out of place.

It has to be organized. This thought is not supported by the facts because the room is organized except for a few out-of-place things. This is an example of the *should* thinking error. Kody exaggerated how important it is for his room to be perfectly organized, even at the expense of enjoying himself sometimes.

I won't feel right until it is done. This thought is not supported by the facts because Kody was able to have fun with his friend instead of working on his room. This is an example of the *overestimating* thinking error.

Once Kody tested his thoughts against the facts, he revised his thinking to be more realistic—seeing the room as organized and not requiring him to do much straightening and arranging. He felt relaxed as a result. In order to help you with testing and revising your thoughts, you can fill out the same form Kody did. Use the Test and change Your Thoughts form on page 66 to help identify, test, and revise your thoughts.

Test and Change Your Thoughts: Kody

			Situation: My room			
Step 1	Step 2	Step 3	Step 4	Step 5	Step 6	Step 7
Thoughts	How Much I Believe The Thought 0-100%	Fear Rocket Rating 1-10 of How I Feel	Facts That Support Thought/Facts That Don't Support Thought	Revise How Much I Believe Thought 0-100%	What Is A Realistic Way to Think About The Situation?	Revise Fear Rocket Rating 1-10 of How I Feel Now!
It's a mess. **Filtering**	100%	10	A few things are out of place. Bed is made. Laptop closed. Books in backpack.	30%	The room is organized. Only a few things are out of place.	3
I can't stand it. **Catastrophizing**	100%	10	I like things organized. I've had more things out of place before. It is nice to have things arranged perfectly!	30%	I can deal with a few things out of place.	3
It has to be organized. **Should**	100%	10	There is no such thing as perfect. Having things organized makes it easier to find things.	30%	It's OK to have the room be mostly organized.	3
I won't feel right until it is done. **Overestimating**	100%	10	I had fun with my friend instead of working on my room. When things are messy, I like to make them neater.	30%	I had fun and felt OK.	3

Test and Change Your Thoughts

Write down each specific thought that you have about the situation. Try to identify the thinking error. Test and revise each individual thought. With practice, the better you'll become at changing thinking errors and becoming a more realistic thinker. Most important, changing your thoughts will help you to feel better.

Situation:						
Step 1	Step 2	Step 3	Step 4	Step 5	Step 6	Step 7
Thoughts	How Much I Believe The Thought 0-100%	Fear Rocket Rating 1-10 of How I Feel	Facts That Support Thought/Facts That Don't Support Thought	Revise How Much I Believe Thought 0-100%	What Is A Realistic Way to Think About The Situation?	Revise Fear Rocket Rating 1-10 of How I Feel Now!

Test Predictions

Another useful way to change exaggerated thinking about the likelihood of bad things happening is through *testing predictions*. You can do this by treating your overestimating thinking error like a prediction and testing it as though you are a scientist. You have to find evidence to support your prediction. The best place to look for evidence about the future is the past—the past is the best predictor of the future!

For example, Fiona *predicts* that she will get sick from her dog because of the flea and tick medicine. She believes 100 percent in her prediction. Taking a scientific view of this statement, she can ask questions to discover whether the evidence from the past supports the prediction.

> *What happened in the past when I petted my dog?*
>
> *Have I ever gotten sick in the past when I petted my dog?*
>
> *How many times have I petted my dog in the past without getting sick?*
>
> *What exactly happened in the past when I petted my dog?*
>
> *Did I pet my dog in the past without getting sick?*

When Fiona answered these questions, she found that she actually never got sick after petting her dog. The evidence or facts did not support her prediction. By testing her prediction and finding no facts to support it, Fiona revised the chances of getting sick from petting her dog to less than 10 percent! As a result of thinking more realistically about getting sick, it will now be easier for Fiona to practice petting her dog. Her dog will be much happier too!

Test Predictions

In the space provided, write down one overestimating thought. Pretend you are a scientist or detective and ask questions that they would ask. Then answer those questions with evidence and facts from the past.

My overestimating (exaggerated) thought:

_____

_____

_____

_____

_____

Scientific questions:

_____

_____

_____

_____

_____

_____

_____

_____

_____

Evidence and facts based on past experience:

_____

_____

_____

_____

_____

_____

Conduct Action Experiments

Another way to learn to be more realistic about how you look at situations is through *action experiments*. This is exactly what scientists do to test predictions. In addition to looking at the past for the evidence, you actually set up an experiment for yourself to see what happens.

Fiona wanted to learn to think more realistically, so she set up an experiment to test her prediction that she will get sick from petting her dog. Here is what she did:

Fiona's Action Experiment

Steps to Take	My Beliefs, Actions, and Outcome
Write down the prediction: What exactly do I think will happen?	*When I pet the dog I will get sick from the flea and tick medicine.*
Rate how much you believe it.	*I believe this will happen 100%.*
Describe an experiment that would test the prediction.	*One day after the flea and tick medicine has been applied to the dog, I will pet the dog's head once.*
Get a helper to assist doing the experiment.	*Mom put the medicine on the dog to help me do the experiment.*
Carry out the experiment.	*I pet the dog once on its head.*
Record the results.	*I felt OK after I petted the dog. I did not get sick.*
Revise the belief in your thought.	*I believe that I will get sick from my dog's flea and tick medicine: 10%.*

By carrying out the experiment, Fiona has gathered evidence that does not support her prediction. She didn't get sick. Now she can revise the thought and change what she actually does. She doesn't have to avoid petting her dog, nor does she have to wash after she pets the dog. Fiona and the dog are much happier!

Now it's your turn to play scientist again. Fill out the form on the next page and record your results!

My Action Experiment

Follow the steps to test your predictions.

Steps to Take	My Beliefs, Actions, and Outcome
Write down the prediction: What exactly do I think will happen?	
Rate how much you believe it.	
Describe an experiment that would test the prediction.	
Get a helper to assist doing the experiment.	
Carry out the experiment.	
Record the results.	
Revise the belief in your thought.	

ABCDs of Fearful Thinking | 71

Stand Up to Bad Outcomes

This technique is a very powerful action to take against the *catastrophizing* thinking error. When you catastrophize, you exaggerate how bad something would be if it happened. You blow things up out of proportion and you exaggerate your *inability to cope* with bad outcomes. Xena is the girl we read about who avoids brushing her teeth and washing her hair. Xena catastrophized when she thought that something very bad could happen that would change her life if she cleaned her teeth. Standing up to bad outcomes involves asking yourself the following six questions:

1. *What would be so bad if what I am thinking actually happens?*

2. *Would it be as bad as I am saying in my head?*

3. *Bad things have happened before—were they as bad as I thought they would be?*

4. *If what I am saying did happen, would I be able to cope with it?*

5. *I have dealt with difficult situations before and didn't I survive?*

6. *Isn't it true that dealing with tough situations can help you learn and get stronger?*

Xena can use this technique to help with the mistaken idea that something terrible would happen if she washed her hair. You can see how Xena did this in the chart below. By asking herself questions to help *stand up* to her thoughts about her life changing permanently, she learns to think more realistically about the situation, that it isn't as bad as she thinks, and that she actually can deal with washing her hair. Standing up to bad outcomes helps to develop a different point of view about situations. It also helps to give yourself more credit for being able to deal with situations that may not go your way. It happens to all of us in life. When things don't go our way, sometimes facing the situation is how we learn and grow.

Here's how Xena stood up to bad outcomes:

Catastrophic Thought	Standing Up to the Bad Outcome	My Ability to Cope
Something terrible will happen if I wash my hair, and I'm afraid it will change my life.	*What's the worst that will happen if I wash my hair? I could slip on the shampoo suds and hurt myself and maybe never walk again. But I have washed my hair before without a problem. Having dirty hair makes my scalp itchy and my hair greasy. I don't like it. I would like to have clean hair.*	*It might not wash my hair as often as other people, but I really like the feeling of clean hair. I felt uncomfortable for a little while, but it went away. Every time I wash my hair I am less worried that something bad will happen. I am learning to be more flexible when I can't control what happens next.*

Catastrophic Thought

Now it's your turn. Write down your catastrophic thought. Next, go back to the six questions from page 71 to stand up to bad outcomes, and write down your responses. Then write how you will cope.

My catastrophic thought:

_____

_____

Standing up to the bad outcome:

1. _____

2. _____

3. _____

4. _____

5. _____

6. _____

My ability to cope:

_____

_____

_____

_____

_____

_____

Slice the Pie

When the OCD Trickster makes you exaggerate your responsibility for bad things happening, it leads to an over-responsibility thinking mistake. The slicing the pie technique can help avoid this error in thinking.

For example, Laney believes that she is responsible for protecting her family from harm, and if anything happens to them she believes that she is responsible. She worries every day about her family's health and worries even more about them when they are not home. When her brother broke his ankle bicycling, she blamed herself because she thought she didn't protect him. The pie chart below shows that Laney took 100 percent responsibility for her brother's injury. This is an example of the over-responsibility thinking error.

Instead of serving the whole pie to yourself, learn to slice the pie to develop a more realistic view of causes and responsibility for events. Here are the five steps of this technique that Laney followed.

Step 1: Describe the situation in detail. Laney explained that she was bicycling with her brother in their neighborhood when he crashed his bike into a tree, fell, and broke his ankle. She ran to her brother to help him. People from the neighborhood came to help get her brother and his bicycle out of the street. She called home for her father, who carried her brother home. Her parents then drove her brother to the hospital. He had a cast put on his broken ankle and returned home.

Step 2: Identify the thoughts you have about what happened. Laney said that she could have watched her brother more carefully and stopped him from riding into the tree.

Step 3: Write down all the possible the causes for the situation. Laney came up with a list of possible causes for her brother's bicycle accident:

- Laney not watching out for her brother.

- A teenager was texting on her phone when she drove by them on the street.

- Her brother was learning how to ride his new bicycle.

- The curvy road.

- Potholes in road.

Step 4: Slice the pie according to how much each cause contributed to the event. Using the list of causes, Laney sliced the pie according to how much each cause was responsible for the accident. You can see this on the following pie chart.

Step 5: Revise your thinking about your responsibility. Looking at the pie slices, Laney realized that she was not the only one responsible for her brother's accident.

The chart below shows how Laney sliced the pie to show how much each cause could have contributed to the accident. The slicing the pie technique helped Laney to develop a more realistic view of her brother's bicycle accident. Taking most of the blame for it didn't make sense when she thought about all of the factors that could have been responsible.

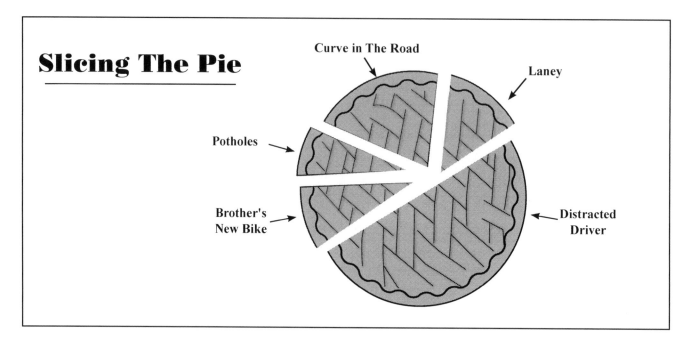

It is important to realize that there are almost always many causes for events. To give yourself most of the responsibility for something bad happening is not realistic. Think about it. Would it make any more sense to give yourself all the responsibility for something good happening?

What You Learned about Changing Fearful Thinking

On the next page is a checklist of the **actions** you learned about in this chapter for identifying and changing fearful thinking. As you learn more about the different types of OCD in the chapters ahead, you'll see how you can use these **actions** for changing your thinking to **beat**, **control**, and **defeat** the OCD Trickster.

Slicing The Pie

Let's try this exercise for one of your thoughts. Grab a pen and follow the five steps for slicing the pie.

1. Describe the situation in detail.

_____

_____

_____

_____

2. Identify the thoughts you have about what happened.

_____

_____

_____

_____

3. Write down all the possible the causes for the situation.

_____

_____

_____

_____

4. Slice the pie according to how much each cause contributed to the event.

_____

_____

_____

5. Revise your thinking about your responsibility.

_____

_____

_____

Worksheet

Errors of Thinking Checklist

Keep a tally of your thinking errors, and check off every action you try to correct the mistaken thoughts.

Types of Errors	✓
Overestimating	
Over-responsibility	
Catastrophizing	
Filtering	
Shoulds	
Superstitious or magical thinking	
Black-and-white thinking	
Fortune telling	
Mind reading	
Thought-action confusion	
How to Change Thinking Errors	✓
Test and revise your thinking	
Test predictions	
Conduct action experiments	
Stand up to bad outcomes	
Slice the pie	

Chapter 6

ABCDs for
Contamination OCD

ABCDs for Contamination OCD

Contamination obsessions and compulsions occur very frequently among people who have OCD. For some people, it may be the only type of OCD that they have. For others, they may have several different types of obsessions and compulsions, with just some of them focused on contamination. Whether your OCD involves a little or a lot of contamination fear, this chapter will help you to focus on **actions** to **beat**, **control**, and **defeat** contamination OCD. You will learn about:

- Stories of contamination obsessions and compulsions

- Types of contamination OCD

- The contamination vicious circle

- **Actions** to **beat**, **control**, and **defeat** contamination OCD

Stories of Contamination Obsessions and Compulsions

It is very common for people with contamination OCD to experience more than one type of contamination obsession. The stories of individuals dealing with contamination obsessions and compulsions show how complicated their fears and worries can be.

Gemal's Story

Gemal is the boy who avoids going near some of his classmates at school because he thinks that their bad luck will rub off on him. His contamination obsession about his classmates has grown to include people outside of his school who he perceives as having problems, bad luck, or some type of disability or limitation. When he sees or goes near people he considers to be contaminated, he feels very worried that their problems will hurt him or his family in some way. As a result, it is very difficult for Gemal to go to school and to other public places. Because he has linked certain locations in his town and neighborhood with the people he perceives to be contaminated, he tries to entirely avoid going to these places. Even seeing pictures or hearing about these people and places causes Gemal to feel contaminated. He is avoiding more and more things as he gives in to what the Trickster tells him to worry about. He doesn't go on the Internet to chat with his friends, he no longer watches television, and he even avoids his family because they talk about people or places that he considers to be contaminated.

From the beginning, Gemal has tried to avoid contact with people, places, or things that he considers to be contaminated. When he thinks that he has been contaminated, he avoids wearing those clothes or belongings unless they have been washed or cleaned. He throws away or stores some belongings that he finds too contaminated. He washes his hands frequently, and he takes showers at night that can last more than 2 hours. He also washes and cleans ritualistically, counting the number of times he washes so that it adds up to what he thinks is a *good number*. When he hears words referring to contaminants, he asks the speaker to "take it back" so that he can feel decontaminated.

Serena's Story

Serena is a girl who has contamination obsessions about body products, the body's private parts, chemicals, animals, animal waste, and public places of any kind. She feels a deep uneasiness when she comes in contact with things that she considers to be contaminated. She says that she just "doesn't feel right." Using the toilet, shower, and bathroom sink and faucet in her own home is difficult because she thinks there is contamination from urine and feces. She has difficulty touching her own private parts because she considers them contaminated. Even a bird sitting on a ledge outside of her window causes her to worry because of bird poop. She tries to avoid all contaminants and washes her hands many times throughout the day to rid herself of the uneasy feeling. The skin on her hands is red, dry, and rough from too much washing.

Clarissa's Story

Clarissa is a girl who has contamination obsessions about flowers and plants that could be poisonous and words and images that are linked to the devil. On vacation with her parents, she became frightened about certain flowers that the tour guide identified as poisonous. Since that trip, Clarissa tries to avoid any contact with flowers and plants unless she gets reassurance that they are not dangerous. When she comes in contact with anything she considers contaminated, she changes her clothes, washes, and showers. She can change her clothes as many as 15 times a day. Clothes that she considers contaminated are avoided and sometimes discarded. Even hearing the word "devil" can cause her to feel contaminated and to change her clothes.

The contamination obsessions that Gemal, Serena, and Clarissa are experiencing include many different types of obsessions, compulsions, and feared consequences. Exposure and response prevention— a.k.a. learning to fly the Fear Rocket to a safe and controlled landing—can be applied to all types of contamination OCD. And there is more help in Chapter 11 for contamination obsessions about God, religion, sin, and the devil.

Types of Contamination OCD

There are many types of obsessive-compulsive contamination behaviors. It is possible for anything, any person, or any situation to be considered a contaminant by someone with OCD. The Trickster can make you believe anything and everything is contaminated. The most common obsessions about contaminants are shown in the list below.

Contamination Obsessions

- **Body fluids and parts:** urine, feces, spit, blood, nose fluid, semen, hair, skin tissue, fingernails, private part, breasts, buttocks

- **Natural environment:** plants, flowers, grass, water, soil, air

- **Environmental contaminants:** chemicals, household cleaners, cleansers, soaps, construction materials, asbestos, dry wall, paint, lead, poisons, pesticides

- **Germs and dirt:** viruses, bacteria, dirt, dust, lint, sticky things

- **People:** people who are sick, people with disabilities, people associated with contaminated places or situations, people seen as having problems or bad luck, people who are poor, people perceived as unattractive, people seen as different

- **Animals and things related to animals:** pets, wild animals, dead animals, insects, animal body parts, animal waste, animal tracks

- **Places and locations:** public places, public restrooms, grocery stores, doctors' offices, department stores, dressing rooms, cemeteries, rooms in homes, areas of rooms, towns, cities, areas of towns and cities

- **Objects, pictures, words, images:** things associated with a contaminant, pictures or words linked to contaminants, mail, newspapers, money, objects in public places or at home, public library books, websites

Decontaminating Compulsions

The 10 major categories of decontaminating compulsions are shown below.

1. **Washing:** washing your body or parts of it, hand washing, showering, wiping, using antibacterial products, washing clothes and belongings

2. **Cleaning:** cleaning room, house, or belongings; vacuuming; using special cleaning products or cleansers

3. **Ritualized washing and cleaning:** washing or cleaning a certain number of times or in a certain order, licking, wiping off or blowing on things

4. **Throwing things away:** throwing objects or personal belongings away

5. **Changing clothes:** dressing and undressing repeatedly, shaking out clothes

6. **Avoidance:** staying away from objects, people, places, and situations that are seen as contaminated; storing contaminated objects in special places or containers

7. **Magical compulsions:** using special phrases, words, numbers, or images to decontaminate objects, people, places, or situations

8. **Wearing or using protective clothing or gear:** wearing gloves or special clothing, using paper towels, using shirt sleeves to avoid contact with contaminants

9. **Reassurance seeking:** asking others for reassurance about danger from contact with contaminants, asking about the effectiveness of using decontaminating compulsions

10. **Protecting others:** safeguarding others from contact with contaminants by using any of the decontaminating compulsions

Feared Consequences

If you have contamination obsessions and decontaminating compulsions, it is very important to ask yourself what it is that you fear. What would happen if you came into contact with a contaminant that you fear? Not everyone with contamination OCD fears sickness or illness. Just as there are many different contamination obsessions and compulsions, there are many different types of scary consequences associated with contamination OCD. The Trickster uses different fears to get people to do compulsions.

Types of Feared Consequences

These are the main types of feared consequences:

- **Physical harm:** disease, sickness, disability, death

- **Psychological or social harm:** change in personality or identity, change or loss in one's life or family, loss of social status or friends

- **Spiritual harm:** punishment by God, being linked to evil and the devil

- **General uneasiness:** feeling that things are not right, that they just don't feel right.

To **beat**, **control**, and **defeat** contamination OCD, you can use the lists of contamination obsessions, decontaminating compulsions, and types of feared consequences to identify what you have been experiencing. If you haven't already, use the My Daily Diary worksheet on page 180 to record your obsessions and compulsions—and what triggers them—for at least one week.

The Contamination Vicious Circle

Malcolm is a boy who avoids eating at school because he is afraid of being poisoned. He also avoids eating any food that has been touched by anyone except himself. Malcolm's fears about being poisoned and getting sick from germs on his food are causing him to worry so much that he is having difficulty eating normally. He doesn't eat all day at school. He can't buy his lunch at school because he is afraid it could be poisoned. He can't bring lunch from home to eat at school because he fears that germs from other students could get on his food. He can't even buy packaged food out of the vending machines to eat. He thinks that there are germs everywhere in the school, in and on the vending machines, in the cafeteria, on the cafeteria tables, in the hallways, in the classrooms, on the desks, on the doorknobs, on his books, on his binders, on his backpack, on his clothes, on his hands, and everywhere he goes in his school.

Malcolm is caught in the OCD vicious circle. The OCD Trickster has grabbed hold of Malcolm's brain and is really faking him out. The Trickster is telling Malcolm to be afraid of getting sick from eating food because it has poison or germs in it. As a result, Malcolm can only eat when he has prepared the food himself and when no one else has come near his food. You can see Malcolm's contamination vicious circle in the next diagram. Malcolm's obsession that the food is contaminated leads him to avoid eating with anyone else, even his own family!

The more he gives in to what the Trickster tells him, the stronger and stronger the Trickster is getting, and the weaker and weaker Malcolm is becoming. Malcolm can use the ABCDs to break out of the contamination vicious circle. He has to fly in the Fear Rocket by confronting the feared consequence of getting sick from food.

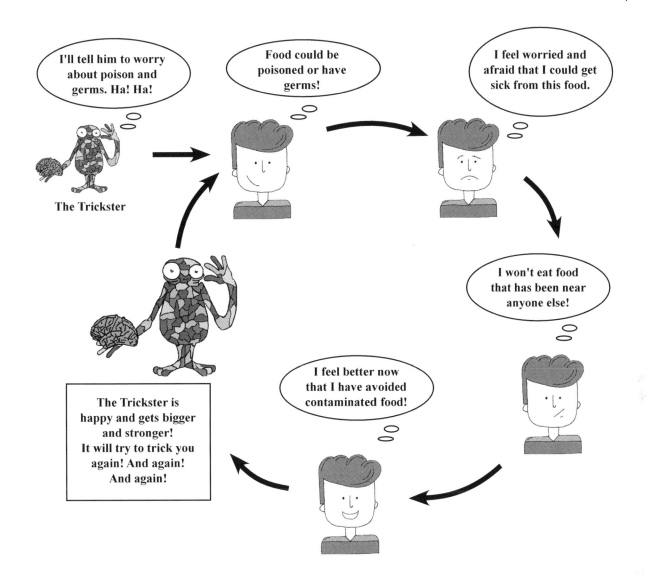

Exposure Exercises: Flying the Fear Rocket

The first step in breaking out of the OCD contamination vicious circle is to identify all contamination behaviors. Based on his OCD Daily Diary, Malcolm identified his contamination obsessions and compulsions, rated each of them from 1 to 10 on the Fear Rocket, and then ordered them from easiest to hardest to face. Malcolm's list is shown on the next page.

Malcolm can use his list to start carrying out ERP exercises for his contamination OCD. At each step along the way, *repeated* exposure to those situations will make it easier and easier to fly the Fear Rocket through the clouds of worry and fear. The Fear Rocket will come down faster and faster for a safe and controlled landing. This is the key **action** for successful exposure and response prevention against contamination OCD.

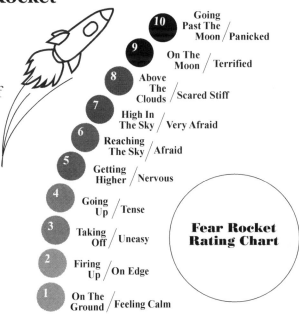

It is important to begin exposures with the easier items on the list. This helps you to build confidence as you work up to the more difficult items. When Malcolm tackles the more difficult items, he can use some of the other tools from Chapter 3 to help him carry out his exposure exercises.

Malcolm's List of Contamination Obsessions and Compulsions/Exposure and Response Prevention Action List

#	Obsessions and Compulsions	Fear Rocket Rating
1	Eating food from the school cafeteria while sitting next to others at the table.	10
2	Eating food by myself that is purchased in the school cafeteria.	10
3	Eating food bought from the school vending machine.	10
4	Drinking water purchased from the school vending machine.	9
5	Eating food at school that was brought from home.	9
6	Drinking bottled water at school that was brought from home.	8
7	Reducing the number of times I use antibacterial wipes.	7
8	Eating food prepared by mother while sitting with my family at the table.	6
9	Eating food prepared by my mother.	5
10	Using door knobs at school without washing my hands afterward.	5
11	Eating fruit touched by a family member.	4
12	Touching school books and binders without washing my hands afterward.	4
13	Drinking and eating from dishes touched by my family.	3
14	Drinking from a glass not washed by me.	2
15	Eating food I prepared while sitting next to my family at the kitchen table.	1

Here are the steps Malcolm followed when he started ERP:

1. On the day Malcolm decided to start flying in the Fear Rocket, he began with the *easiest* item on his list: eating food he had prepared while seated next to family at the kitchen table. He found this exposure easy, so after a few days he began eating his food at the table with the rest of his family.

2. Next he tackled drinking from a glass that he had not personally washed. At first Malcolm felt a little afraid, but he encouraged himself by *telling himself* that he didn't have to listen to the Trickster trying to fool him, and that he could fly the Fear Rocket through the clouds of worry to a safe landing. He succeeded.

3. Malcolm then challenged himself to drink and eat from dishes touched by his family. Malcolm felt afraid at first, so he had his family touch the dishes with only one finger, then two, then three, then four, then five, until he was able to have them hold dishes with both of their hands (he took *small steps,* thereby changing the compulsion *a little at a time*). With the encouragement of his family, he was able to fly in the Fear Rocket through the fear to a safe landing.

4. Next Malcolm tried touching schoolbooks and binders without washing his hands afterward, rated 4 on the Fear Rocket. The Fear Rocket flew higher in the sky for this exposure. Malcolm felt very worried that he could get sick, but he reminded himself again that he *didn't have to listen* to the OCD Trickster. He pushed himself to fly the Fear Rocket.

5. He used *small steps* to tackle the exposure of eating fruit touched by a family member, also rated 4 on the Fear Rocket. First he had his mother touch an apple with just her pinky, and then she added one finger at a time for Malcolm's *exposure practices*. Eventually his mother was able to hold the fruit in her whole hand and hand it to Malcolm to eat.

6. Moving on to using doorknobs in school without washing afterward, Malcolm used a variety of tools to help with the exposure. He used *positive self-talk, rehearsed doing the exposures in his imagination, practiced* on door knobs at home, and changed the compulsion *a little at a time*. When he touched a door knob he *delayed* washing for 15 minutes while he went about his activities. He also encouraged himself by thinking of all of his friends at school who touched the door knobs freely and didn't have problems as a result. Using these tools, he eventually stopped the washing completely.

7. Eating food prepared by his mother was also rated 5 on the Fear Rocket. *Little by little* Malcolm worked his way up to eating home-cooked meals. At first he ate simple foods: cut-up fruit, cereal with milk, soup, and then macaroni and cheese. By *reducing* the compulsive avoidance *a little at a time,* he grew comfortable eating all food prepared by his mother—except for peas, which he never liked!

8. Next he tackled eating meals prepared by his mother while sitting at the table with his family. First he sat at the table by himself while *imagining* eating his meal with his family. Then he sat at the table during a meal for a few minutes (*small steps*). With the *repeated practice* of staying at the table longer, he eventually succeeded in eating full meals at the table with his family.

9. Malcolm moved on to the next Fear Rocket item: reducing the number of times he used antibacterial wipes. In his Daily Diary he had counted using 20 wipes a day. He began fighting the OCD Trickster by stopping the use of wipes in his own room, then other rooms in his house, then in school, and then in restaurants and other public places. Eventually he stopped using the wipes entirely.

10. Drinking water in school, rated 8 on the Fear Rocket, was the next item Malcolm tackled. Again, he *rehearsed this in his imagination* before actually doing the exposure. Although difficult at first, when he actually drank water in school, he flew the Fear Rocket through the fear to a safe landing.

11. Eating food in school, rated 9 on the Fear Rocket, was a very difficult item for Malcolm to tackle. Once again he began by taking *small steps*. He brought a sandwich in a plastic bag to school so that he could eat the sandwich *a little at a time* without taking it completely out of the bag. Getting used to eating in school took time and *many practices*, but he became increasingly comfortable and happy about being able to relax with his friends in the cafeteria. He really felt relief that he didn't have to listen to the OCD Trickster!

12. Over time, Malcolm moved on to buying bottled water out of the school vending machine. He encouraged himself by using *self-talk*, and he discovered that this exposure wasn't as hard as he thought it would be. With all of his success, he felt ready to take on the more difficult items on his list.

13. Malcolm challenged himself to eat food in school purchased from vending machines and the school cafeteria. He prepared for this exposure by *encouraging himself, rehearsing the exposure in his imagination,* thinking about *what his friends do,* and getting *a helper to practice* with him in the cafeteria when no one was around.

14. He flew the Fear Rocket higher than ever before by eating food purchased in school at the cafeteria table. He *practiced* this in his *imagination* and *rehearsed* it at home. He did it first by himself during a free period with the *help of his guidance counselor*. He then did the exposure during a normal lunch period.

15. With all of his success, Malcolm felt confident about eating food from the school cafeteria at the lunch table with his friends. Although he worried a lot about this exposure, he flew the Fear Rocket and succeeded in carrying out the top exposure on his list. Malcolm was happy that he was **beating, controlling,** and d**efeating** contamination OCD! He *rewarded* himself for his hard work! He broke out of the contamination vicious circle!

Changing Fearful Thinking about Contamination

In addition to repetition of exposures and the other actions Malcolm used as he worked his way down his list, Malcolm helped himself to **beat** contamination OCD by *changing his thinking*. The goal of changing thoughts is to think more realistically. He *tested and revised* his thoughts about contamination by examining the facts.

Look at the form on the next page to see how Malcolm tested and revised his thinking. Malcolm thought that food prepared by others or eaten near others was dangerous because it could have poison or germs in it. By testing his thoughts, Malcolm realized that he was *overestimating* the chances of getting sick from food. He also realized that if he did get sick it wouldn't be that bad. He realized that when he was sick in the past he got better! He can *stand up to a bad outcome*!

When Malcolm ate a piece of fruit that had been touched by a family member, he *tested the prediction* that he would get sick. When he didn't get sick, he revised his prediction. But what if he had gotten sick? He would have used the *slice the responsibility pie* technique to identify all the possible causes for getting sick. Malcolm would have then revised his thoughts about the causes for getting sick to be more realistic.

Situation	My Thoughts - What is Going Through My Head?	How Much I Believe Thought 0-100%	Fear Rocket Rating 1-10	Facts That Support Thought / Facts That Don't Support Thought	Revise How Much I Believe Thought 0-100%	What Is A Realistic Way to Think about The Situation?	Revise Fear Rocket Rating 1-10
Eat food prepared by my mother	Food could be poisoned. **Overestimating**	95%	5	One time I got sick and threw up after I ate dinner at home. My family has eaten hundreds of meals cooked by my mother, and everyone is healthy.	20%	I am *overestimating* the likelihood of food being poisoned. Food cooked at home is safe.	2
Eat my food from home in school.	Germs could get on my food and make me sick. **Overestimating**	99%	8	Kids at school get sick sometimes. I have eaten in school many times and never got sick.	40%	I am *overestimating* the chances of getting sick from getting germs on my food. I am making a bigger deal out of it than it is. I am catastrophizing. Even when I have been sick in the past, I got better. Getting sick isn't as bad as I am making it out to be! I can *stand up to bad outcomes*!	3

Actions to Beat, Control, and Defeat Your Contamination OCD

Now you can start to use the ABCDs for contamination OCD. To do this you will need to:

1. **Identify obsessions and compulsions.**
   Use this chapter's list of contamination obsessions and compulsions to help identify your contamination behaviors. Identify what it is that you fear. Keep track of your OCD contamination behaviors for a few days using the My Daily Diary in the Appendix.

2. **Rate your behaviors on the Fear Rocket and list them from high to low.**
   Record your list in the chart My List of Contaminations and Obsessions in the Appendix.

3. **Do exposure exercises—fly the Fear Rocket!**
   Plan exposure exercises. Begin by filling in the chart to **beat**, **control**, and **defeat** Contamination OCD on the following pages. Use the actions explained in this chapter and in Chapter 4 to help yourself do exposures. Carry out exposures beginning with items lowest on your list.

4. **Change mistaken thoughts about contamination.**
   Identify mistakes in thinking about contamination that you learned about in Chapter 5. Use the Test and Change Your Thoughts worksheet (in the Appendix) to work on making your thinking more realistic.

How to Beat, Control, and Defeat Contamination OCD

Use this form to practice the ABCDs of OCD.

1. Write down what the OCD Trickster tells you to worry about.
2. Tell yourself that you know it's the Trickster talking to you trying to scare you.
3. Tell yourself that there is no real reason to be afraid.
4. Tell yourself that you don't have to listen to the Trickster.
5. Tell yourself that you can ride the Fear Rocket safely back down to the ground.
6. Tell yourself that you are getting stronger and the Trickster is getting weaker.

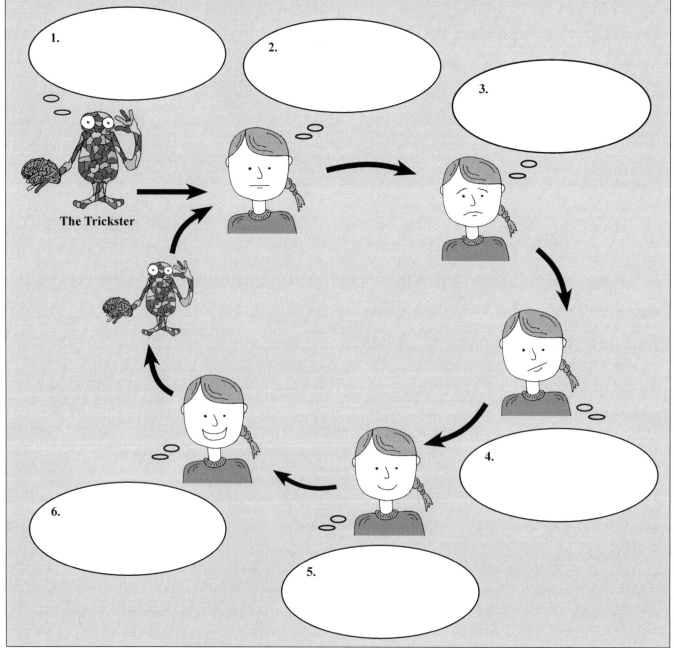

How to Beat, Control, and
Defeat Contamination OCD

Use this form to practice the ABCDs of OCD.

1. Write down what the OCD Trickster tells you to worry about.
2. Tell yourself that you know it's the Trickster talking to you trying to scare you.
3. Tell yourself that there is no real reason to be afraid.
4. Tell yourself that you don't have to listen to the Trickster.
5. Tell yourself that you can ride the Fear Rocket safely back down to the ground.
6. Tell yourself that you are getting stronger and the Trickster is getting weaker.

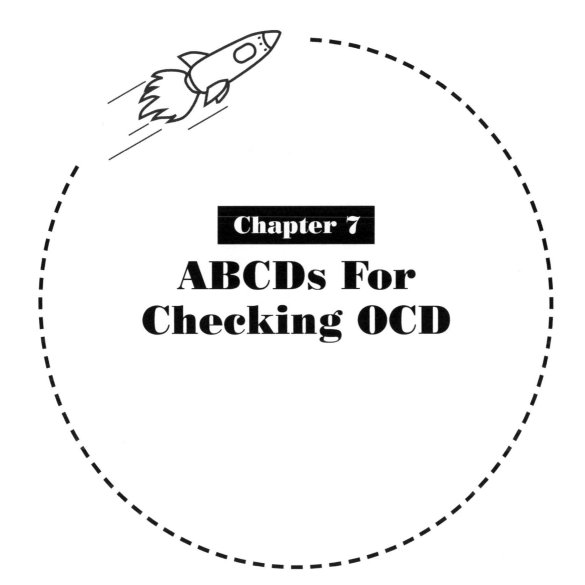

Chapter 7
ABCDs For Checking OCD

ABCDs for Checking OCD

Checking obsessions and compulsions are another common type of OCD. This chapter can help you to **beat, control**, and **defeat** checking OCD. You will learn about:

- Stories of checking obsessions and compulsions

- Types of checking OCD

- The checking vicious circle

- **Actions** to **beat**, **control**, and **defeat** contamination OCD

Stories of Checking Obsessions and Compulsions

The stories of individuals dealing with checking obsessions and compulsions show that they worry about whether they have done something wrong or carried out some action incompletely or unsatisfactorily. They worry excessively about doing something incorrectly that could lead to something bad happening.

Hayley's Story

Hayley is a girl who asks her parents over and over again to repeat what they said in order to be sure she heard them correctly. She wants to be certain that she knows information exactly. She fears that if she makes a mistake she will be criticized or punished. At school she repeatedly raises her hand to ask the teacher questions about what was said. She asks her friends questions again and again to make certain that she understands what they said. She also questions them to find out whether they understand what she said. Her family, teachers, and friends get impatient with Hayley because of her excessive reassurance seeking. She has tried to ask for less reassurance by writing down information and the answers she gets from her questions. She keeps a special notebook that she checks repeatedly to be sure that she remembers what she has written. Hayley finds it very difficult to relax and enjoy herself because of constant worry about knowing information exactly. She has a difficult time completing school assignments because she worries about understanding what the teacher assigned. She checks and rechecks her day planner to be sure she understands the assignment. She worries that there is something wrong with her because she can't remember everything that was said.

Will's Story

Will calls his mother many times during the day to make sure that she is safe. He worries so much about the safety of his family that he checks windows, doors, locks, curtains, sinks, faucets, the stove, the oven, and the lights to make sure that everything is shut off and closed. Before he goes to bed at night he checks everything several times to be certain that things are off, closed, or locked. It is a very tiring routine, but he does it because he feels very anxious until he has completed his checking. Sometimes he goes to bed late because he avoids starting his checking because he knows it will take him a long time to finish it. If he is interrupted in his checking he has to repeat the checking again until he feels it is done right. Will even gets up in the middle of the night to make sure that everything is okay. He is afraid that something bad could happen to him and his family if he doesn't do his checking. Will gets especially worried when he goes away for a day or more. He checks the heat lamps for his pet lizards 10 or more times to make sure they are working properly. He worries about the house burning down or flooding because he didn't check enough. He fears that his dog and cat might die if they couldn't get out. It is very difficult for Will to leave home. He dreads going away on vacation because of the anxiety.

Rashida's Story

Rashida is very worried about making a mistake that would be disapproved of by others. She spends excessive time checking everything she does to make sure that she did not do something wrong. She thinks that it is terrible to make a mistake of any kind. If she does something wrong she thinks that she will be rejected by others because she is a bad person—a loser who doesn't deserve anything in life. She checks everything she does to make sure that no one will disapprove of her or reject her. She thinks that her parents would think less of her and not love her as much if she does something incorrectly. She is also anxious about putting bad words or comments in anything that she writes. When she writes messages to her friends on the computer or assignments for school, she triple-checks to make sure she didn't put any bad words or comments in what she has written. When she is walking to and from school, going from one classroom to another, or even going from one room to another at home, she looks back repeatedly to see if she dropped anything or left anything behind. She fears that something she left behind could get her into trouble. She is very afraid that others will think she is a bad person. Sometimes she even thinks that she could be arrested and put in jail for writing something or doing something bad.

Types of Checking OCD

The stories of Hayley, Will, and Rashida show that people with checking OCD have excessive worry about causing any kind of harm or damage for which they would be responsible. The main obsessions and compulsions they have are shown in the list below. Checking obsessions are focused on harm, danger, and safety. Checking compulsions are done to prevent harm and damage of any kind.

Checking Obsessions

- Fear that you could be harmed by: physical injury, pain, or illness; psychological or emotional injury or pain; or spiritual suffering or pain

- Fear that you could harm others by causing: physical injury, pain, or illness; psychological or emotional hurt, injury, or pain; or spiritual suffering or pain

- Fear that you could harm animals

- Fear that you could damage your own property or belongings

- Fear that you could damage other people's property or belongings

Checking Compulsions

- Checking to prevent harm to yourself

- Checking to prevent harm to others and/or to assure yourself that no harm occurred

- Checking to prevent harm to animals and/or to assure yourself that no harm occurred

- Checking to prevent harm to property or belongings and/or to assure yourself that no harm occurred

- Checking to prevent harm to others' property or belongings and/or to assure yourself that no harm occurred

- Checking to make sure that you completed something, that you did something correctly, or that you understand something

Feared Consequences

The Trickster makes people with checking OCD excessively concerned with making mistakes and being held responsible for them. People with checking OCD experience excessive doubt and uncertainty about whether they have done something, or whether they have done it well enough. The main types of feared consequences are shown below.

Types of Feared Consequences

- **Punishment:** being physically punished, losing privileges, having things taken away

- **Self-blame or guilt:** feeling bad about causing harm, not doing enough to protect yourself, others, animals, or property

- **Social disapproval:** being criticized or viewed by others as bad or incompetent

- **Spiritual harm:** being punished by God

- **Viewing yourself negatively:** seeing yourself as a failure, a loser, lazy, stupid, crazy, a bad person, and so on

To **beat**, **control**, and **defeat** checking OCD, you can use the lists of checking obsessions, compulsions, and feared consequences to identify what you have been experiencing. To do this, use the My Daily Diary (see page 34) of your obsessions and compulsions for a week. Pay particular attention to what triggers your obsessing and what you fear would happen if you don't perform a checking compulsion. Write this down in your My Daily Diary worksheet.

The Checking Vicious Circle

Ernesto is the boy with checking OCD that you learned about in Chapter 2. He checks everything in his room at night before he goes to bed: the lights, windows, computer, cell phone, curtains, closet, door, and underneath the bed. He checks everything over and over until he feels that they're right. You can see the checking vicious circle Ernesto was caught in on page 12. The more Ernesto did what the Trickster told him, the more and more he checked. He even began checking kitchen appliances and the windows, doors, and lights in the rest of his house. His checking took so long to do that he went to bed later and later at night. He sometimes fell asleep in school the next day because he was so tired from checking.

What is it that Ernesto fears? The Trickster grabbed hold of Ernesto's brain to make him worried about his safety, the safety of his family, and the safety of his pets. The Trickster tells Ernesto to worry about people breaking in to his house at night if the doors and windows are not shut and locked. Because his bedroom is the first room at the top of the stairs he fears that any intruders would go after him first to hurt him. He worries that his house could catch fire if the lights and appliances are not shut off. He even checks the wires from his computer and cell phone because he is afraid they could catch fire if they are too close to the heat.

Exposure Exercises: Flying in the Fear Rocket

Based on his OCD Daily Diary, Ernesto identified all of his checking obsessions and compulsions, what triggered them, and what he feared would happen. He rated them from 1 to 10 on the Fear Rocket and listed them from low to high.

Ernesto's list of Obsessions and Compulsions

#	Obsessions and Compulsions	Fear Rocket Rating
1	Check doors and locks once.	10
2	Check garage and basement once.	10
3	Don't check windows in house.	9
4	Do not check on parents in their bedroom or ask them for reassurance.	8
5	Don't check stove and kitchen appliances.	8
6	Do not check inside closet before bed.	7
7	Do not check under bed before going to sleep.	6
8	Plug in cell phone and don't check again.	6
9	Do not check light switches in all the rooms of the house.	5
10	Turn lights off once in my bedroom and don't check.	4
11	Shut off computer once and don't check.	4
12	Set alarm clock once and don't check.	4
13	Close my bedroom curtains once and don't check.	3
14	Shut off lamp next to bed and don't check again.	2
15	Don't check electric plugs in electrical outlets in room.	1

10 — Going Past The Moon / Panicked
9 — On The Moon / Terrified
8 — Above The Clouds / Scared Stiff
7 — High In The Sky / Very Afraid
6 — Reaching The Sky / Afraid
5 — Getting Higher / Nervous
4 — Going Up / Tense
3 — Taking Off / Uneasy
2 — Firing Up / On Edge
1 — On The Ground / Feeling Calm

Fear Rocket Rating Chart

Ernesto can now use his list to carry out exposure and response prevention exercises for his checking OCD. Beginning with the items rated lowest on the Fear Rocket, he can practice doing ERP by resisting what the OCD Trickster tells him to do. Each time he stops himself from carrying out a compulsion,

Ernesto will get stronger and the Trickster will get weaker. Repeating the exposures will make it easier and easier to fly in the Fear Rocket to a safe landing. When he succeeds with an item, he can move on to the next highest item on his list.

Here are the steps Ernesto followed for doing his ERP on his list of items.

1. On the first day of doing ERP, Ernesto decided that he would not check to see if everything was properly plugged into the electrical outlets in his room. Usually he would check all the outlets in his room by holding the plug and pushing it once or twice into the outlet. This would take him a few minutes to complete. He worried that there could be a fire if a plug was not pushed all the way into the outlet. He *told himself* that *no one else in his family worried* about plugs and that *there had never been a fire*. He felt confident about his ability to stop checking the plugs and very pleased that he *resisted listening to the OCD Trickster*.

2. Next, Ernesto was able to shut off the lamp next to his bed just once—without turning it on and off two to three more times to make sure that it was really turned off. This was a little difficult at first, but he *talked back to the Trickster* and, after a few days of *practicing* flying in the Fear Rocket, he didn't feel much of an urge to perform the checking compulsion. When he turned the lamp off once, he went to sleep.

3. Before going to sleep, Ernesto usually closed the curtains on his window very carefully. He would get up a couple of more times to check to see that they were closed completely so that no one could see into his room. He feared that people would break into the house and know where to find him because they could see him in his room. Using *self-talk*, Ernesto told himself that he had closed the curtains well the first time so he didn't need to check them again. Saying out loud, "The curtains are closed," helped. After a few days of flying in the Fear Rocket, his worry about checking the curtains went away. He felt very good about his ability to **beat** the OCD Trickster.

4. The next item, setting the alarm clock without checking, was a little more challenging. Ernesto would usually set the alarm clock, then check several more times to make sure it was on the right wake-up time for the morning. He worried that he would get up too late in the morning, miss the school bus, and get into trouble. Although difficult for Ernesto, he managed to face up to the OCD Trickster by doing a *gradual exposure* when he set the alarm clock. He reduced the checking in *small steps*. After setting the clock, he first reduced his checking to three times. After succeeding with that he reduced it to twice, then to once, and then to no checking at all.

5. Shutting off the computer without checking was also a more difficult challenge for Ernesto. Ernesto was afraid that the computer could catch fire during the night if left on. He used self-talk to remind himself that the computer was on during the day and did not catch on fire. He used a gradual exposure technique to help himself fly in the Fear Rocket by reducing his checking from three times to no checking at all.

6. Turning off the lights without checking was also challenging. Ernesto feared that if the light switch was not completely in a down position, it could start a fire inside the wall. Using self-talk and a gradual exposure technique, Ernesto reduced his checking. He told himself that no one else worried about the light switches. Seeing that the light was off meant that the switch was in the off position. Saying out loud that the light switch was off also helped.

7. Once Ernesto was able to stop checking the light switches in his room he also succeeded in reducing his checking of light switches in other rooms of his home.

8. Before Ernesto went to sleep, he plugged in his cell phone for recharging. He checked repeatedly to make sure that the phone was plugged in and that the wires for the phone were not near the heat in his room. He feared that a fire could start from the plug not being in the phone the right way or from the wires being too close to the heat. He used realistic thinking and a gradual exposure technique to stop checking the electrical outlets in his room. He told himself that there had been no fire even though no one else in his family checked like he did. He also recognized that no one else he knew had a cell phone catch on fire. Using realistic thinking and gradually reducing his checking, Ernesto succeeded in stopping the checking of his cell phone.

9. Before going to sleep, Ernesto checked under his bed three to four times to see if there was someone there who could hurt him. Ernesto's parents helped him to reduce his checking in small steps. Eventually he stopped looking under his bed before going to sleep.

10. Once Ernesto stopped checking under his bed, he found it somewhat easier to reduce checking inside his closet. Within a few days of practice, he completely stopped this checking compulsion.

11. To stop checking the stove and kitchen appliances, Ernesto reduced his checking one step at a time for each appliance, beginning with the toaster. He reduced the number of times he checked it from four to three to two to one—and then to no checking at all. He then worked on the coffeepot and, finally, the stove. Eliminating this checking routine was difficult. Ernesto also carried out an action experiment; the results showed Ernesto that nothing caught fire even though he didn't do his checking. Eliminating this checking routine built his confidence to tackle his higher Fear Rocket items.

12. Before going to bed, Ernesto always checked to see that his parents were safe in their bedroom, including asking them if everyone else in the house was okay. He would ask them several times for their reassurance. Again, Ernesto reduced this checking compulsion in steps—and with repeated practice stopped it completely. He then completely stopped going into their room.

13. With the help of his parents, Ernesto also reduced checking windows in the house in a gradual way, from four to three to two to one—to none. This was very difficult for Ernesto, so he practiced this first in his imagination. With repeated practice day after day after day, he rode the Fear Rocket to a safe and controlled landing.

14. By the time Ernesto got to the highest items on his list, he felt very good about his ability to beat the OCD Trickster. Because checking the garage and basement were rated high on the Fear Rocket, he planned to do it in stages and to allow himself to check it once before going to bed. He used realistic thinking to help do the exposures. He succeeded in doing this and then went on to eliminate checking the garage and basement completely.

15. Checking the doors and locks in the house only once was also very difficult. Having succeeded with all the other items on his list, Ernesto had confidence about gradually reducing his checking from six to five to four to three to two to one—and then to none. Finally, Ernesto was free from listening to the OCD Trickster! Free of unrealistic worrying, Ernesto was much happier and enjoyed the time he had for himself before going to bed. This was a great reward for breaking out of the checking vicious circle.

Changing Fearful Thinking about Checking

Ernesto helped himself to **beat** checking OCD by changing his fearful thinking to be more *realistic*. Look at the form on the next page to see how Ernesto tested and revised his thinking. Ernesto feared that he could be responsible for a fire breaking out in his house. This fear led him to do excessive checking of electronic devices, light switches, and electric appliances. When he reviewed the facts, he realized that he was *overestimating* the chances of appliances or electronic equipment causing a fire. He also realized that the responsibility for protecting his family did not belong to him alone. Based on the facts, he revised his fearful thinking to be more realistic and felt less afraid as a result.

The OCD Trickster also caused Ernesto to fear that people could break into his house and harm him and his family. Ernesto's compulsive checking of his bed, his closet, curtains, windows, the basement, the garage, and doors and locks were done to make sure everyone would be safe. By *testing and revising his thinking* obsessions about safety, harm, and danger, as well as *slicing the responsibility pie* about his responsibility for protecting himself and his family, Ernesto helped himself to *think more realistically* about the risk of people breaking into his house. This helped him to reduce his fear and his compulsive checking. He **beat** back the OCD Trickster!

Test and Revise My Thoughts: Ernesto

Situation	My Thoughts - What is Going Through My Head?	How Much I Believe Thought 0-100%	Fear Rocket Rating 1-10	Facts That Support Thought / Facts That Don't Support Thought	Revise How Much I Believe Thought 0-100%	What Is A Realistic Way to Think about The Situation?	Revise Fear Rocket Rating 1-10
Don't check stove and kitchen appliances	Appliances will catch fire, house will burn down, and then my family will be hurt. **Overestimating** I'll be responsible. **Over responsibility**	100%	10	My mother says that it is good to unplug electrical appliances when they aren't being used. There has never been a fire in our house even though the oven was left on one time. Appliances have been left plugged in overnight without a fire.	10%	The chances of the stove or kitchen appliances causing a fire are low.	3
Don't check windows, garage, basement, doors, and locks.	People will break in to our house and hurt me and my family. **Overestimating**	100%	10	There are reports on TV of people breaking in to houses. My parents told me that they watch over the family and our house so that I am not the only one concerned about safety. There have been no break-ins in our neighborhood.	10%	My family has lived in this neighborhood for many years and there has never been a break-in.	3

Actions to Beat, Control, and Defeat Your Contamination OCD

Now you can start to use the ABCDs for checking OCD. To do this you will need to:

1. **Identify obsessions and compulsions.**
   Use this chapter's list of checking obsessions and compulsions to help identify your checking behaviors. Identify what it is that you fear. Keep track of your OCD checking behaviors for a few days using the My Daily Diary worksheet in the Appendix.

2. **Rate your behaviors on the Fear Rocket and list them from high to low.**
   Record your list in the chart My List of checking obsessions and compulsions in the Appendix..

3. **Do exposure exercises—fly the fear rocket!**
   Plan exposure exercises. Begin by filling in the chart to beat, control, and defeat checking OCD on the following pages. Use the actions explained in this chapter and in Chapter 4 to help yourself do exposures. Carry out exposures beginning with items lowest on your list.

4. **Change mistaken thoughts about checking.**
   Identify mistakes in thinking about checking that you learned about in Chapter 5. Use the Test and Change Your Thoughts worksheet (in the Appendix) to work on making your thinking more realistic.

How to Beat, Control, and Defeat Your Checking OCD

Use this form to practice the ABCDs of OCD.

1. Write down what the OCD Trickster tells you to worry about.
2. Tell yourself that you know it's the Trickster talking to you trying to scare you.
3. Tell yourself that there is no real reason to be afraid.
4. Tell yourself that you don't have to listen to the Trickster.
5. Tell yourself that you can ride the Fear Rocket safely back down to the ground.
6. Tell yourself that you are getting stronger and the Trickster is getting weaker.

The Trickster

How to Beat, Control, and Defeat Your Checking OCD

Use this form to practice the ABCDs of OCD.

1. Write down what the OCD Trickster tells you to worry about.
2. Tell yourself that you know it's the Trickster talking to you trying to scare you.
3. Tell yourself that there is no real reason to be afraid.
4. Tell yourself that you don't have to listen to the Trickster.
5. Tell yourself that you can ride the Fear Rocket safely back down to the ground.
6. Tell yourself that you are getting stronger and the Trickster is getting weaker.

The Trickster

ABCDs For Perfectionism OCD

Chapter 8

ABCDs for Perfectionism OCD

Perfectionism obsessions and compulsions are a problem for many people with OCD. This chapter can help you to **beat**, **control**, and **defeat** perfectionism OCD. You will learn about:

- Stories of perfectionism obsessions and compulsions

- Types of perfectionism

- The perfectionism vicious circle

- **Actions** to **beat**, **control**, and **defeat** perfectionism OCD

Stories of Perfectionism Obsessions and Compulsions

Individuals dealing with perfectionism OCD try to live up to unrealistic standards of behavior and achievement. They worry excessively about failing or falling short in their effort to meet their impossible goals.

Tammy's Story

Tammy is the girl who gets to school late every day because she has to get cleaned up and dressed so perfectly that it takes a lot of time to get herself ready. She has to catch her school bus a block away from her house at 8:30 in the morning. She sets her alarm clock for 5:30 a.m. because it takes her a full three hours to get herself ready to leave the house. Even before she goes to bed at night she spends a full hour getting her clothes ready for the next morning. She carefully picks out the clothes, tries them on, and checks how they look in the mirror. She has such difficulty deciding what to wear that she will go through many outfits before settling on one that she likes. Once she has picked out her clothes, she lays everything out in the order that she will put them on in the morning.

When she has trouble picking out her clothes for the next day, she ends up going to bed late. Even when she has had less sleep than she needs, she still gets up when her alarm goes off at 5:30 a.m. She takes a shower that can last as long as an hour because she has to wash and rinse carefully to be sure she is perfectly clean. She takes another hour to dry and brush her hair, brush her teeth, and look at her face in the mirror for any type of blemish. She will redo her hair several times if even one hair seems out of place. Tammy then gets dressed slowly and carefully. She checks how she looks in the mirror so much that she doesn't finish getting dressed until it's almost time to catch the school bus. She grabs something to eat on her way out the door. Even though she's tired all day long from her night and morning routines, she does the same thing every single day in order to make sure she looks as perfect as possible. She is afraid that she won't be liked and popular if she doesn't look attractive.

Peter's Story

Peter worries about damage occurring to any of his belongings. A small nick or defect that no one else would notice causes Peter a great deal of worry. When he gets new clothing of any kind, he puts it away carefully in his drawers or closet so that it will be safe. He doesn't wear the new clothes he buys or receives as gifts because he likes to keep them new and unused for as long as possible. Sometimes he

105

keeps his clothes for so long without wearing them that he grows out of them. He has had a new lacrosse stick stored in his closet for six months because he wants to keep it new and undamaged. When he buys things in the store, he checks them over for a long time to make sure that they are not damaged or flawed in any way. When he brings new clothes home, he checks them again. If he finds a thread hanging off the shirt, even on the inside where it can't be seen, he will bring it back to the store. If the clothing can't be returned to the store, he will throw it away because he can't stand the idea that it is not perfect.

Peter guards all his belongings from any type of damage. He doesn't allow anyone in his family or any of his friends to touch any of his things. He checks his cell phone and his computer frequently to make sure there is no mark on them. He cleans them very carefully even when he doesn't find any dirt. He doesn't like anyone coming into his room because he worries that he or she will damage his belongings. As a result, he worries when he is out of the house and unable to watch over his belongings. At school, he watches over his belongings in his locker and backpack to make sure no one touches them or damages them. If anyone does touch any of his things, he checks them over to make sure they haven't been dirtied or damaged. He can't stand the thought of anything happening to his belongings that would make them less than perfect.

Clevados's Story

Clevados spends several hours during the day making sure everything around her is properly arranged and organized. Everything in her room has to be in a very specific place. If something is moved out of place she feels very anxious until she places it back exactly where it belongs. "Everything has a place, and everything in its place," is a guideline she always tries to follow. All of the clothes in her dresser drawers are meticulously folded and placed carefully in the drawers according to color and type of clothing. Clothes are hung in the closet in the same organized way, each item of clothing separated by two inches from other items. Items on top of the dresser are lined up and arranged in specific places. The books in the bookcase are arranged by size and placed exactly one and one-half inches from the edge of the shelf. Items on top of Clevados's desk are lined up evenly. Her computer is placed exactly in the center of the desk. She cleans the desk off and repositions all the objects on the desk before beginning to work at her desk. When she opens up files on her computer, if she doesn't feel that they have been opened correctly, she closes them and reopens them until it feels right. Clevado's computer files are arranged alphabetically and by color. Papers are filed in her binders according to color-coded tabs with the name of the subject typed onto the tab. Clevados keeps lists of all homework that has been completed or assigned. She checks and updates these lists and rewrites them if they are not neat enough. She saves all completed assignments in binders labeled by subject and organized by date. She stores these binders in labeled boxes kept under her bed. She spends so much time arranging and organizing her things that she has very little time for fun.

Types of Perfectionism OCD

The stories of Tammy, Peter, and Clevados show that people with perfectionism OCD hold themselves to extremely high standards and are driven to try measuring up to them. Despite the goals being impossible to fulfill, they continue to pressure themselves to meet their excessively high standards. It is important to understand the difference between normal standards and perfectionistic ones. It is normal to care about personal hygiene and looking our best; it is not normal to spend so much time on our appearances that it interferes with other activities. It is normal to take care of our belongings; it is not normal to protect our things so much that we don't use them or share them appropriately with others. It is normal to try to be organized; it is not normal to spend so much time organizing things that it interferes with getting on with what we are supposed to do. Perfectionistic standards are extreme, unreasonable, and rigid. Normal standards are moderate, reasonable, and flexible.

Perfectionism Obsessions

- **Overconcern about yourself:** worry about personal hygiene, grooming, appearance, or clothes

- **Overconcern about your performance:** worry about speaking, writing, grades, athletic performance, popularity, or performance evaluations of any kind

- **Overconcern about your belongings:** worry about preserving things as new or protecting things from damage or wear and tear from normal use

- **Overconcern about your environment:** worry about order, neatness, balance, and organization

Perfectionism Compulsions

- **Slowness:** carrying out actions very slowly to make sure they are correct or right

- **Checking:** repeatedly going over actions, work, or performance to make sure there are no errors and to correct mistakes

- **Redoing:** erasing or crossing out writing, or rewriting or retyping

- **Repeating:** carrying out actions over and over until they are correct or feel right

- **Reassurance-seeking:** repeatedly asking others to review your work, your performance, or your understanding to make sure that what you have done or think is accurate, exact, correct, or free from error

- **Procrastination:** delaying or postponing tasks because of worry about not doing well or of failing to live up to an extremely high standard of performance

- **Indecisiveness:** inability to make choices or taking too long to make them because of worry about not making the correct decision

- **Overdoing:** worry about not doing things correctly or completely, which causes behavior such as being overly thorough in speech, writing, organizing, or list-making.

Feared Consequences

The Trickster makes people with perfectionism OCD overly concerned and worried about living up to unrealistic, if not impossible, standards of behavior and performance. The main types of feared consequences are shown below.

Types of Feared Consequences

- **Viewing yourself negatively:** seeing yourself as a failure, unworthy, weak, defective, unfit, stupid, or incompetent

- **Having your behavior or performance viewed negatively:** being criticized, reprimanded, corrected, rated poorly, or graded low

- **Social disapproval:** being rejected, considered unpopular, or viewed as unattractive, unfit, or socially awkward

- **Feeling uncomfortable:** feeling out of control or unable to act because of the inability to stop doing compulsive behavior

To **beat**, **control**, and **defeat** OCD, you can use the lists of perfectionism obsessions and compulsions, and feared consequences, to identify what you have been experiencing. To do this, use the My Daily Diary (see page 180) of your obsessions and compulsions for a week. Pay attention to what triggers your obsessions and what would happen if you don't do a perfectionistic compulsion. Record your observations in the My Daily Diary worksheet.

The Perfectionism Vicious Circle

Brooke is the girl with perfectionism that you learned about in the introduction. She is overly concerned with doing everything absolutely correctly. She spends hours during the day making lists of what she has to do, repeatedly checking and rewriting her lists to make sure that she is up to date with everything. She worries a great deal about doing her absolute best in school. She wants to please her parents and her teachers by getting A's on all her work. If she gets anything less than an A, even an A-, she considers it a failure and thinks that she won't be able to get into a good college. When she writes in class, she is extremely careful about her penmanship. If she makes a small mistake in even one letter in a word, she has to erase the whole word and rewrite it. Because of her erasing and rewriting, she often misses out on what the teacher says. Brooke is so concerned about understanding and remembering what she has read that she rereads everything several times. This makes it very difficult to finish reading even short reading assignments. As a result Brooke has fallen behind in her work. Knowing that it will be hard to live up to her extremely high standards, she puts off starting assignments. She waits so long to start her work that she is often unable to get assignments done when they are due.

What is it that Brooke fears? The Trickster has grabbed hold of Brooke's brain to make her afraid that she will perform less than perfectly, make mistakes, and be criticized. She can't stand the thought of getting anything wrong. She is afraid of being seen as a failure in her own eyes and the eyes of others. Her drive to be perfect is actually interfering with her ability to do her work. She is spending so much time on writing and rewriting lists, going over her lists, checking her work, and rereading and rewriting that she has fallen further and further behind in her work. Because it is impossible for Brooke to live up to her rigid and unrealistic standards, she worries more and more and procrastinates more and more.

Exposure Exercises: Flying the Fear Rocket

Brooke began to **beat** the OCD Trickster by using the My Daily Diary to help identify her perfectionism behaviors. She identified her obsessions, compulsions, triggers, and what she feared would happen if she didn't do her compulsions or compulsive avoidance. She rated each of the behaviors on the Fear Rocket.

10 Going Past The Moon / Panicked
9 On The Moon / Terrified
8 Above The Clouds / Scared Stiff
7 High In The Sky / Very Afraid
6 Reaching The Sky / Afraid
5 Getting Higher / Nervous
4 Going Up / Tense
3 Taking Off / Uneasy
2 Firing Up / On Edge
1 On The Ground / Feeling Calm

Fear Rocket Rating Chart

Brooke's List of Perfectionism Obsessions & Compulsions

#	Obsessions and Compulsions	Fear Rocket Rating
1	Begin working on assignments sooner so that they can be completed by the due date.	10
2	Reduce checking answers on tests.	9.5
3	Reduce time spent deciding how to answer test questions.	9
4	Reduce rereading.	8.5
5	Reduce erasing, crossing out, and rewriting.	8
6	Reduce asking parents to check my work.	7.5
7	Leave less early to arrive for school and other appointments.	7
8	Reduce checking the school website for current and future assignments.	6.5
9	Reduce checking completed homework assignments.	6
10	Reduce repeatedly checking with teacher to make sure I understand what he said.	5.5
11	Reduce asking parents for reassurance.	5
12	Reduce repeating what I say to make sure others understand.	4.5
13	Reduce checking to-do list.	4
14	Don't rewrite to-do list.	3
15	Check graded homework only once.	2

Brooke can begin practicing to fly in the Fear Rocket by doing exposure and response practices with the easier items on her list. By not doing what the OCD Trickster tells her to do, Brooke will fly in the Fear Rocket to a safe and controlled landing. With repeated practice, she will get better and better at **beating**, **controlling**, and **defeating** the Trickster, and become less and less perfectionistic.

Here are the steps Brooke took for practicing ERP on her list of items.

1. For her first practice, Brooke chose to beat the Trickster by *reducing the number of times* she checked her graded homework. When she got graded work back from the teacher, Brooke went over it a few times. She worried that she wouldn't understand what the teacher wanted her to do unless she studied her answers and how they were graded. For her *exposure practice*, Brooke read a returned assignment only once. Although she was a little worried, she *told herself* that it would be okay.

2. Brooke tackled her next item by *resisting* the compulsion to rewrite her to-do list. This was a little difficult for her, but she *encouraged herself* and practiced *talking back* to the OCD Trickster.

3. It was more difficult for Brooke to *reduce* checking the to-do list. She would usually check it five or more times per day to make sure that she knew what assignments were due. She worked on this

exposure by reducing checking the list one less time per day (*gradual exposure*). By *repeatedly* flying in the Fear Rocket through her worry, she grew comfortable with checking her to-do list fewer and fewer times until she was okay with checking it once in the morning and once at night.

4. Brooke's family and friends complained about her tendency to repeat what she said in order to make sure they understood her. Brooke *enlisted her family to help* **beat** her compulsive repeating. She agreed that her family would signal her any time that she started to repeat what she had said so that she could stop herself. Although difficult for Brooke to do, the *assistance of her family helped* Brooke to become more aware of the compulsive repeating. It also helped that her family gave Brooke an opportunity to do her repeating at scheduled times (*make an appointment with the obsession*). Having this outlet helped her to fly the Fear Rocket through her worry about not being understood.

5. Brooke's *family* also *helped* her to reduce asking for reassurance. Brooke asked for reassurance about nearly everything, including whether she had done something right, whether she should do something, and whether she had hurt someone's feelings. At first, Brooke's family and friends told her that they would answer her only once when she asked them for reassurance. Further attempts for reassurance would be ignored. This was difficult for Brooke to deal with in the beginning. She used *distraction, relaxation skills*, and *techniques to change her thinking* to help her fly in the Fear Rocket. Although it took longer to do than the easier items on the list, Brooke eventually succeeded in reducing her requests for reassurance. And as she got better, Brooke also asked her *best friend to help* by not giving in to her reassurance requests.

6. Building on her success, Brooke tackled the compulsive checking with her teacher. She would repeatedly raise her hand in class to ask her teachers questions about what they said. Teachers and students were growing impatient with Brooke's repeated questioning. To **beat** this compulsion, Brooke asked her *teachers* to help her reduce her questioning. She wrote down her questions during class and either asked them after class, after school, or through email. The number of questions she was allowed to ask was also gradually reduced. With lots of practice, Brooke eventually reduced her questions to only a few per week.

7. Next Brooke practiced reducing her checking of completed homework. She did this *gradually*. To help **beat** the Trickster, she worked on *changing her thinking* to reduce her worry about flying the Fear Rocket. She also *talked to her friends* about how often they checked homework. With *repeated practice* she checked and worried less. She actually had more free time to do fun things.

8. Brooke used *gradual exposure* to stop repeated checking of homework and other future assignments posted on the school website. She *asked her friends* how many times they checked the website. She used her My Daily Diary to keep track of her checking and reduced it to one less time every other day until she checked it twice per day. She also carried out an *action experiment* that showed her reduced checking did not result in a poor grade.

9. Leaving very early to arrive at school and appointments was a difficult compulsion for Brooke to tackle. She didn't want to be late for anything because she feared disapproval and punishment. She reduced the compulsion *gradually* by leaving a few minutes later for school each day. *She kept track* of her arrival times in her Daily Diary. This was a difficult exposure exercise and required a lot of repetition for Brooke to become less worried about being late.

10. Brooke found it more difficult to stop asking her parents to check her work. She *tested and revised her thinking* to be more realistic. She asked her parents to check her work twice, once while she worked on it and once when she finished (*gradual exposure*). In the past she would ask them to

check on it many times. When she succeeded with this she tried asking for help only when she did not understand something and only when she needed help proofreading something she had written.

11. Brooke's erasing, crossing out, and rewriting interfered with completing assignments on time. For Brooke to work efficiently and get things done, she needed to reduce these compulsions. She *broke down this difficult exposure into parts*. She began by practicing not erasing while writing about things unrelated to schoolwork. She wrote letters to her family and friends as practice. Next she tried writing *pretend* homework without erasing and rewriting. She moved on to writing without erasing and rewriting homework in her strong subjects, such as math. *Gradually* she was able to write or type homework without doing any erasing, crossing out, or rewriting. Eventually she was able to practice doing this with all her written work, flying the Fear Rocket without giving in to compulsive rewriting.

12. Completing reading assignments was very difficult for Brooke because she reread the material so many times. She couldn't finish reading books on time. She used a *gradual exposure* technique to reduce rereading. To begin, she did the exposures with reading not assigned in school. With the *help of her parents* she agreed to reduce her rereading a *step at a time*. She *practiced* reading one sentence without rereading, then two, then three, and so on until she could read a whole paragraph without rereading. When she succeeded with this she *practiced* with school assignments.

13. Brooke found it difficult to complete tests within the time limit given because of the excessive time she spent trying to decide on how to answer questions. She worried about failing to answer the question the way the teacher wanted it answered. As a result, she was given permission by teachers to have additional time to complete tests. Brooke preferred taking the tests during normal class times and wanted very much to work on **beating** this compulsion. She began by doing *exposures in her imagination* and working on *changing her mistakes in thinking*. Next she practiced by *pretending* that homework assignments were actual tests. Her *parents coached* her in *reducing the time* she spent thinking about how to answer questions. She *pushed herself* to start writing answers after a shorter time thinking, putting pen to paper and starting to write without picking up the pen. When she felt confident about her ability to do this at home, she *practiced* in school on short quizzes by answering questions quicker, putting pen to paper and starting to write without picking up the pen. After a couple of weeks of *practice*, she moved on to doing this with tests. Her progress with this required *lots of practice*, and she worried a lot, but eventually she flew in the Fear Rocket so well that she was able to write answers to questions much quicker than before.

14. Checking answers to questions also made it difficult for Brooke to complete tests on time. For this exposure, Brooke *practiced at home* with her homework, moved on to quizzes, and eventually to tests (*gradual exposure*). **Beating** back the Trickster, Brooke was eventually able to check her answers once and move on. With *repetition* of this exposure practice, she was able to take tests without doing excessive checking.

15. Starting assignments sooner, the item rated highest on the Fear Rocket in Brooke's list, also required Brooke to break the exposure practice down into *small steps*. Brooke would usually worry so much about doing a project that she would avoid doing it until just before it was due. As a result, Brooke was unable to complete longer-term assignments and would often give up doing them entirely. Here are the *steps* Brooke took to **beat** her compulsion to avoid.

   A. Choose topic
   B. Get approval from teacher
   C. Identify one source you need through research online and in the library. Then find a second source, then a third, and so on
   D. Read and take notes on each source

  E. Write outline to identify main topics and subtopics
  F. Write out ideas for each topic and subtopics
  G. Write first paragraph
  H. Write second paragraph, then third, fourth, and so on
  I. Have parents check first draft
  J. Submit first draft to teacher for review
  K. Review draft with teacher
  L. Write the final draft and submit on due date

Once Brooke identified all the steps above, she wrote down a *date* by which *to complete* each of the *steps* in order for her to finish the entire project by the due date. Brooke and her parents had an agreement that she would limit checking with them—reporting her progress to them at each step along the way to get feedback on what she had done. Following the schedule was difficult; it meant flying the Fear Rocket through her perfectionistic worries, but her success in **beating** the Trickster on all the other items in her list helped her to push through to complete the project successfully by the due date.

Changing Fearful Thinking about Perfectionism

Brooke helped herself to **beat** her perfectionism OCD by changing her thinking to be more realistic. The form on the next page shows how Brooke identified and changed some of the unrealistic thinking that caused her to avoid doing her work. She revised the *overestimation* that she wouldn't understand what the teacher wanted and that she would get a bad grade. Brooke's mistake in thinking, overestimating, was really causing Brooke to do a lot of her compulsive checking, repeating, reassurance-seeking, and avoiding or procrastinating. *Revising* her overestimates to be more *realistic* helped her **beat** perfectionism OCD. Brooke also greatly exaggerated the negative effects of making mistakes or getting grades lower than an A. By asking herself to *stand up to a bad outcome* she also beat the OCD Trickster.

She also tested her thought that she wouldn't know when she had done enough research to be able to write her paper. This thinking reflected the mistaken belief that she *should* know everything about the topic before beginning the paper. Testing this mistaken thinking by *looking at the facts*, she realized that she needed to have only 5 sources and that the teacher said that would be enough information for her to be able to do the paper. Revising her thinking to be more realistic enabled her to stop avoiding and to begin doing her research.

Test and Change My Thoughts: Brooke

Situation	My Thoughts: What is Going Through My Head?	How Much I Believe Thought 0-100%	Fear Rocket Rating 1-10	Facts That Support Thought / Facts That Don't Support Thought	Revise How Much I Believe Thought 0-100%	What Is A Realistic Way to Think about The Situation?	Revise Fear Rocket Rating 1-10
Start work on my project.	I don't know what the teacher expects, and it won't be what he wants. I won't get a good grade. **Overestimating**	100%	10	Sometimes I don't answer questions exactly the way that teachers want, and I lose credit. The teacher told me that I am doing well on the work I have done. I have gotten good grades on homework and tests.	20%	I can earn a good grade on the work that I do.	4
Complete project by the due date.	I have to do complete research before I write the paper. I won't know when I have enough. **Should**	100%	10	I haven't completed projects because I didn't know when I had enough information. The teacher said that 5 sources is enough. I have a schedule for when to finish the research.	20%	I have had trouble in the past, but now I have skills and a plan for doing the research. I can get feedback from my parents and teacher to help me.	4

Actions to Beat, Control, and Defeat Your Perfectionism OCD

Now you can start to use the ABCDs for perfectionism OCD. To do this you will need to:

1. **Identify obsessions and compulsions.**
   Use this chapter's lists of perfectionism obsessions and compulsions to help identify your perfectionism behaviors. Identify what it is that you fear. Keep track of your perfectionism behaviors, including triggers and feared consequences for a week using the My Daily Diary (Appendix).

2. **Rate your behaviors on the Fear Rocket and list them from high to low.**
   Record your list in the My Obsessions and Compulsions worksheet (Appendix).

3. **Do exposure exercises—fly the fear rocket!**
   Plan exposures. Begin by filling in the diagram to **beat**, **control**, and **defeat** perfectionism OCD on the next page. Use the actions explained in this chapter and in Chapter 4 to help yourself plan and carry out exposures. Begin your ERP with items lowest on your list.

4. **Change mistaken thoughts about perfectionism.**
   Identify mistakes in thinking about perfectionism. Use the Test and Change Your Thoughts worksheet (Appendix) to make your thinking more realistic.

How to Beat, Control, and Defeat Perfectionism OCD

Use this form to practice the ABCDs of OCD.

1. Write down what the OCD Trickster tells you to worry about.
2. Tell yourself that you know it's the Trickster talking to you trying to scare you.
3. Tell yourself that there is no real reason to be afraid.
4. Tell yourself that you don't have to listen to the Trickster.
5. Tell yourself that you can ride the Fear Rocket safely back down to the ground.
6. Tell yourself that you are getting stronger and the Trickster is getting weaker.

How to Beat, Control, and Defeat Perfectionism OCD

Use this form to practice the ABCDs of OCD.

1. Write down what the OCD Trickster tells you to worry about.
2. Tell yourself that you know it's the Trickster talking to you trying to scare you.
3. Tell yourself that there is no real reason to be afraid.
4. Tell yourself that you don't have to listen to the Trickster.
5. Tell yourself that you can ride the Fear Rocket safely back down to the ground.
6. Tell yourself that you are getting stronger and the Trickster is getting weaker.

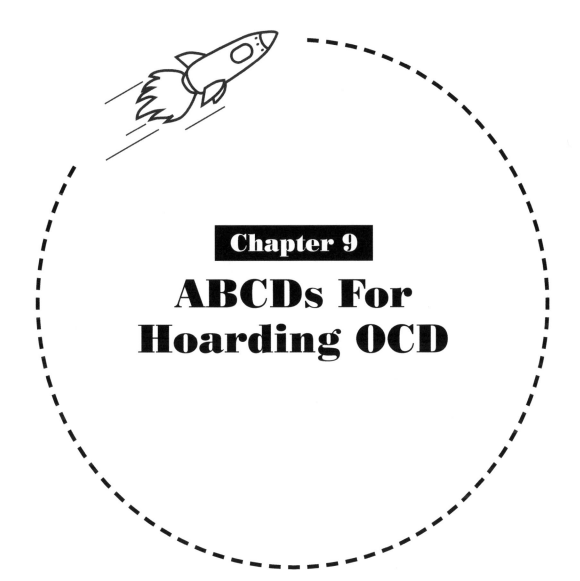

Chapter 9

ABCDs For
Hoarding OCD

Chapter 9

ABCDs for
Hoarding OCD

Hoarding OCD may be mixed in with other types of obsessive-compulsive symptoms. This chapter can help you to **beat**, **control**, and **defeat** hoarding OCD. You will learn about:

- Stories of hoarding obsessions and compulsions

- Types of hoarding

- The hoarding vicious circle

- **Actions** to **beat**, **control**, and **defeat** hoarding OCD

Stories of Hoarding Obsessions and Compulsions

People with hoarding OCD collect and save worthless, useless objects or too many objects. They have great difficulty discarding things and are overly worried about losing or misplacing the things they have saved.

Simon's Story

Simon is a little boy who loves books. He especially likes to collect books about the American Civil War. He takes out many books from the public library. He has also bought many Civil War books with his allowance money. His family gives him gifts as well. His bookcase is overflowing with books, the shelves and the top of the bookcase are filled with books. Because the bookshelf can't really hold any more books, Simon has piles of books on the floor and underneath his bed. His parents are concerned because Simon now keeps piles of books on top of his bed. He is surrounded by books and nearly buried by them when he lies down in his bed. Simon doesn't want any of the books moved off of his bed and gets very upset if anyone tries to move the books. In fact, he doesn't want any of the books in his room moved at all. Despite having so many books, he hardly reads any of them. He might read a few pages at night before he falls asleep. Yet he still wants to go to the library every week to check out more books, even when he hasn't finished reading the ones that he already has.

His parents have now told Simon that he must return books to the library before he can check out new ones. Simon is angry about this new rule. His parents have also removed the books from his bed and floor and put them in boxes in the basement. He is not allowed to pile books on the floor anymore and can have only two books in bed before he goes to sleep. He is very upset about not having all of his books in his room. He can't stop thinking about the books and how much he would like to have them back in his room.

Meredith's Story

Meredith worries about not remembering things so she writes down information in notebooks and on pieces of paper that she saves in her room. When she goes away on vacation with her parents, she uses hotel stationary to write down the names and birthdays of all the new children that she meets. She packs these notes in her luggage to take home with her, even though she knows that she will probably never see these children again. She also brings home napkins, paper cups, plastic utensils, and stacks of travel brochures that she picks up in the lobbies of hotels. Meredith saves these useless keepsakes from all her trips with her family, storing them away in boxes and dresser drawers in her room. She also saves the same kinds of mementos from all the parties and special events that she attends. She has hidden these away in her room for fear that they could be found and thrown out. The thought of losing any of her keepsakes makes her very uncomfortable. She feels as though it would be like losing a part of herself.

Meredith also has a collection of dolls that she keeps in her room. She has recently started to move some of the dolls out of her room because she has started to fear that they might come to life and hurt her and her family. Her parents have reassured her that the dolls cannot come to life, but Meredith is so worried that she doesn't want to be alone in her room with the dolls.

Oberto's Story

Oberto is a boy you heard about in the introduction to this book who picks up scraps of paper and other objects that he finds on the ground. It is hard for him to walk anywhere without stopping to pick up things. He picks up empty paper wrappers, tinfoil, bottle caps, bottles, and just about anything else that catches his eye. He puts the stuff he picks up into his pockets and his backpack. He keeps these things in his locker at school, his backpack, his room at home, and behind and underneath furniture in his house. When his parents found some of the scraps he had hidden, they threw them in the trash can. They couldn't understand why Oberto was saving and hiding stuff that they considered to be garbage. Oberto got very upset when they asked him about it, but he couldn't explain why he collected the things, except to say that he liked the things he picked up and wanted them. When his parents aren't around, he looks through the kitchen garbage to get his stuff back. He really wants his parents to leave his things alone. He can't throw away the things he has collected, and he certainly doesn't want anyone else to throw them out.

Oberto also has difficulty spending money. He receives a weekly allowance that he saves in his own bank account. He likes the idea that he has saved his money and does not want to spend any of it. He is critical of his family for the money they spend, frequently questioning them about whether they are saving enough money. He worries that they could be spending too much money, even though his family is doing okay financially.

Types of Hoarding OCD

The stories of Simon, Meredith, and Oberto show that people with hoarding OCD feel strong urges to collect and save things, even when others would say that the things they save are garbage. It is also clear that they all have difficulty throwing out any stuff that they have collected.

It is important to understand the difference between normal collecting and compulsive collecting and hoarding. Many people collect things as a hobby, such as stamps, coins, shells, paintings, antiques, stuffed animals, baseball cards, model planes, dolls, and even cars. People collect all sorts of things, including unusual items such as the sticky labels on bananas! People who collect things enjoy organizing and displaying their collections. For example, collectors of baseball cards store their cards in specially designed sleeves to protect their cards. They keep track of the cards they own, they attend baseball card shows, and they enjoy looking for new cards to add to their collection. Collecting is an activity that they do for fun, and their collection does not interfere with normal life and everyday activities.

Hoarding OCD is different because it interferes with normal living. Simon's collection of books on the Civil War got to be so large that there was no longer room for him to sleep in his bed. Meredith wasted time collecting information and things that were not useful. Oberto collected things considered garbage and then worried about having them thrown out. He also worried about spending money. Collecting and hoarding interfered with their lives, their living space, their time, their spending, and their families. And it certainly wasn't fun! The OCD Trickster was fooling them into thinking that they had to save, collect, and not throw anything away. Here are some key differences between normal collecting and saving and hoarding:

- Size of collection is too big for the space available

- Items collected are inappropriate: they're useless, worthless, or even considered trash

- Attachment to the items is excessive: parting with them, being away from them, or throwing them away is highly distressing

- Collected items or objects that are not alive are viewed as having life-like feelings and qualities

Hoarding Obsessions

- Worry about having or getting certain things or possessions

- Worry about losing or misplacing things or possessions

- Worry about throwing things or possessions away

- Worry about anyone moving, using, or touching your things or possessions

- Worry about spending money appropriately

Hoarding Compulsions

- Collecting or saving an excessive number of objects that interferes with normal living

- Collecting or saving worthless or useless objects

- Difficulty throwing worthless or useless objects away

- Difficulty sharing or allowing others to handle or touch possessions

- Difficulty spending money appropriately

Feared Consequences

The Trickster makes people with hoarding OCD excessively concerned about collecting useless things, having too many things, not letting others use their things, and not throwing their things away. It is often hard for people with hoarding OCD to realize that their hoarding thoughts and behaviors are not normal. Other people's reactions to the hoarding behaviors are important to take into account in figuring out whether your symptoms are reflect hoarding OCD.

It is helpful to look at the list of feared consequences below to see if any of them apply to you and your experience. Ask yourself what it is that you fear would happen if you didn't get the things you want, if the things you have are lost or misplaced, or if you or others throw out your things. These are some of the common fears associated with hoarding OCD.

Types of Feared Consequences

- Feeling uncomfortable, unhappy, angry, and upset

- Feeling that part of yourself will be lost

- Fearing that you won't be able to forget about lost, misplaced, or discarded possessions

- Worrying that you won't have things, information, or money when you need them

- Worrying that you or your family could be hurt

- Worrying that things or possessions will be damaged

- Fearing that things or possessions will feel bad, hurt, or disappointed

To **beat**, **control**, and **defeat** hoarding OCD, use the lists of hoarding obsessions and compulsions and feared consequences to identify what you have been experiencing. To do this, keep a Daily Diary of your obsessions and compulsions for a week. Pay attention to what triggers your obsessions and what would happen if you don't do the hoarding compulsions. Record your observations in your Daily Diary.

The Hoarding Vicious Circle

Oberto is caught up in the hoarding vicious circle. He is giving in to the OCD Trickster by picking things up off the ground and saving them. What does Oberto fear? He has a difficult time explaining why he picks things up, except that he feels uncomfortable if he doesn't do it. It just doesn't *feel right*. He also feels very strongly about hanging on to the stuff he collects, even if he has to hide it from other people. The thought of his stuff being thrown away makes him upset and angry. His worry about not spending money comes from a different fear. He worries about wasting his money and not having enough. He worries about his family's financial security and whether they will be okay in the future. Despite the fact that his parents have assured him that he can buy some things for himself, and that the family has enough money for their future, Oberto continues to worry unrealistically.

Exposure Exercises— Flying the Fear Rocket

Oberto decided that he would try to **beat** the OCD hoarding Trickster with his family's help and encouragement. He began by keeping a Daily Diary for a week to help him identify his obsessions, compulsions, triggers, and what he thought would happen if he didn't do the hoarding compulsions. He made a list of all of his behaviors and rated each one on the Fear Rocket.

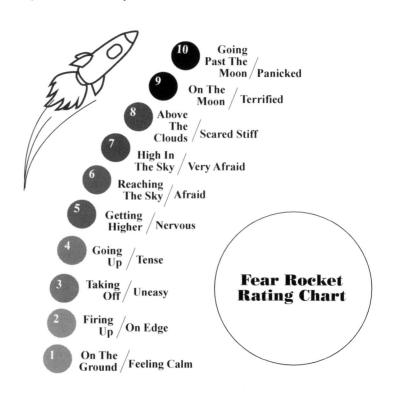

10 Going Past The Moon / Panicked
9 On The Moon / Terrified
8 Above The Clouds / Scared Stiff
7 High In The Sky / Very Afraid
6 Reaching The Sky / Afraid
5 Getting Higher / Nervous
4 Going Up / Tense
3 Taking Off / Uneasy
2 Firing Up / On Edge
1 On The Ground / Feeling Calm

Fear Rocket Rating Chart

Oberto's Exposure Response Prevention Action List

#	Obsessions and Compulsions	Fear Rocket Rating
1	Pick out something new for myself and buy it with my own money.	10
2	Keep some allowance money for myself instead of depositing it in the bank.	10
3	Stop asking my parents about their spending and saving.	9
4	Allow my parents to throw away some hoarding items.	9
5	Throw away sticks and paper from my boxes.	9
6	Throw away bottle caps and tinfoil from my boxes.	8
7	Throw away bottles and cans each day from my boxes.	8
8	Organize new and old hoarding items from home, my backpack, and locker into boxes by type of item.	7
9	Remove all hoarding items from my school locker and backpack.	7
10	Take walks without picking up anything.	7
11	Take a walk without picking up paper.	6
12	Take a walk without picking up sticks and tinfoil.	5
13	Take a walk without picking up bottle caps.	5
14	Take a walk without picking up bottles and cans.	4
15	Put newly collected hoarding items into labeled boxes: bottles, cans, bottle caps, tinfoil, sticks, paper.	3

Oberto challenged himself to **beat** hoarding OCD by tackling the easier items on his list of behaviors. He encouraged himself by *saying to himself* that he didn't have to listen to what the OCD Trickster told him to do. By taking *small steps* and *repeatedly* flying the Fear Rocket, he would get stronger and stronger and the Trickster would get weaker and weaker.

These are the steps that Oberto took for doing ERP on his list of hoarding behaviors.

1. For his first exposure, Oberto asked his parents for six boxes, which he labeled with the names of items he would put into them. Usually when he picked things up off the ground, he would keep them in his room, his backpack, his locker at school, and sometimes hidden in corners and behind furniture. Now he planned on putting new items he picked up into the boxes he had labeled. He would be able to keep track of the stuff he was picking up and eventually know how well he was doing in stopping this compulsion. He used *self-talk*, saying that he didn't have to listen to the Trickster.

2. It was harder for Oberto to do ERP with the next item: stopping himself from picking up bottles and cans on the ground. He *talked back* to the OCD Trickster and *told himself* that he could **beat** it. He *tested and revised* his thinking to make it more *realistic*. He *rehearsed* the exposure. He *practiced*

for a few days around his block. Sometimes he found it so hard that he gave in to the compulsion. But with more practice, the Fear Rocket didn't go up as high, and he was able to succeed by not picking up any bottles or cans. He put the box with the bottles and cans aside because he was no longer adding any more to the box.

3. Oberto used a variety of **actions** to help him stop picking up the bottle caps. He *talked back* to the Trickster, he told himself that *none of his friends* picked up bottle caps. He also used *relaxation* and *distraction* techniques. When he saw bottle caps on the ground that he wanted to pick up, he *refocused* on thinking about something else or *listened to a song* on his music player. It took lots of practice and persistence, but Oberto eventually stopped picking up bottle caps.

4. The **actions** Oberto used to stop picking up bottles, cans, and bottle caps helped him to stop picking up sticks and tin foil. He also broke the exposure into *small parts*. He *rehearsed* in his imagination and then *practiced* exposures when he walked around his neighborhood. When he succeeded, he tried it on his walks to school. He eventually stopped picking up sticks and tinfoil.

5. With the *confidence* he gained from stopping picking up bottles, cans, bottle caps, sticks, and tin foil, Oberto successfully used a variety of **actions** to **beat** the Trickster once again, this time with paper. He broke the exposure practice down into *small steps*. Each day he tried to resist picking up paper. He *rewarded* himself with a point for every time he resisted. His parents agreed to get him a video game when he earned 100 points.

6. Oberto worked hard on stopping the compulsion to pick up things from the ground. With lots of hard work, the use of many *different exposure techniques*, and the *encouragement of his parents*, Oberto **beat** the Trickster by stopping the compulsion to pick up useless things from the ground. It took lots of practice and persistence, but he walks everywhere now without picking up things. He feels very proud of his accomplishment!

7. Moving up his list, Oberto removed all the hoarding items from his school locker and backpack (rated 7 on the Fear Rocket), and put them into the labeled boxes with the other collected items (also rated 7). He felt very worried about taking out his items. He said that looking at his empty locker and backpack made him feel empty. He *tested and revised his thinking* about hoarding these items and *talked back* to the Trickster. Although it was difficult for him to fly in the Fear Rocket, he did succeed.

8. Oberto said that he felt happy that he was able to clear out the items and organize them into boxes. His *parents helped* him to sort out his collected items. He *talked back* to the Trickster and used *self-talk* to encourage himself. This set the stage for the next step of throwing things away.

9. Oberto practiced throwing bottles and cans away by first *rehearsing* it in his mind, *writing out his fear*, and *singing it*! He also *tested and revised his thinking* to be more realistic. He then felt more confident about starting to throw the collected bottles and cans away. Putting them into the recycling bin helped him feel less worried. He broke the exposure down into *small steps*. He threw one away one day, two the next day, three the next, and so on until all of them were gone. He started to feel more and more confident about his ability to **beat** the Trickster and fly in the Fear Rocket.

10. Oberto used the same techniques to throw away the items from the other boxes: bottle caps and tin foil. He *rehearsed, tested and revised his thinking, encouraged* himself, and used his *parents as helpers*. By using *small steps* he succeeded in throwing all the items out.

11. It was more difficult for Oberto to throw out the sticks and paper—rated 9 on the Fear Rocket. Along with the techniques he used to help him throw away the other items, he used the technique of *exaggerating* the obsession. He said that by throwing out the sticks and paper, he would be miserable for the rest of his life, a failure, and always regret that he no longer had the security of the

trash he had collected! By saying this over and over, he actually ended up feeling less afraid. The *exaggerating technique* helped him to see that it was silly to collect such useless stuff.

12. With all the *exposure practice* and throwing things away, Oberto took on allowing his parents to throw away some of the old hoarding stuff. His parents had taken these things from him and stored them because Oberto wouldn't allow them to be thrown out. Oberto used *self-talk*, *rehearsing*, and *singing* out the fear to get ready for the actual exposure. He also used *relaxation techniques* to help himself cope with his worry. When the time came to for his parents to throw away the old hoarding items, Oberto's fear level had come down a lot. He felt good about his success.

13. With the *help of his parents*, Oberto *practiced* not seeking reassurance from his parents about their spending and saving (9 on the Fear Rocket). He slipped many times, but when he did, his *parents* were instructed by him not to answer and to say that it was just the Trickster trying to get him to seek reassurance. Oberto also *talked back* to the Trickster and *tested and revised his thinking* to be more realistic. Oberto greatly reduced the compulsion and then stopped doing it altogether.

14. Keeping some money for himself by not depositing all his money in the bank was a difficult exposure for Oberto. He felt very happy about all the money that he had in the bank and checked his account every day to look at his savings. His *parents helped* Oberto do the exposure in *small steps.* He agreed to keep a small amount of his allowance for himself. He also *tested and revised his thinking* to be more realistic about the need to save all of his money.

15. Oberto agreed to use some of the money he had not deposited in the bank to buy something for himself. His *parents helped* and he also *talked to his friends* about the kinds of things they bought. He approached this in *small steps*. To begin, he went to the store to buy an inexpensive item for himself. Each week he *practiced* buying something for himself until he was finally able to spend a moderate amount of money on something for himself. Oberto felt very good about having reduced his *unrealistic worry* about spending money appropriately.

Changing Fearful Thinking about Hoarding

Changing mistaken thinking to be more realistic can help to **beat** hoarding OCD. Oberto worked on changing some of his unrealistic thinking to help stop doing the compulsive collecting and hoarding. You can see this in the form on the next page. He identified his thought that he had to pick things from the ground as a *should* command from the OCD Trickster. He recognized that he didn't have to do what the Trickster said (*call it by its name*). When he tested the thought that he would miss having the stuff he collected, an *overestimation*, he realized that any discomfort he felt about not picking up the things wouldn't last long. He could fly the Fear Rocket to a safe and successful landing.

Oberto *tested and revised his thinking* about throwing away the things he had collected. He originally thought that the things he collected wanted him to save them and keep them. He identified this as a *magical thinking* or *superstitious thinking* error. He said to himself that his feelings about the things he collected didn't match the facts. The things he collected were not alive and did not have thoughts or feelings. Also, *no one else collected* these kinds of things because they are inappropriate objects. Realizing this, he felt more confident about throwing the hoarding things away.

Oberto tested and revised his thinking about money as well. He really believed that it was very important for him to save all of his allowance money. He felt secure having his money in the bank. Looking at the facts, he identified this as a *black-and-white* thinking error. While saving money is good, it is normal to spend some money and to enjoy buying some things for yourself. He also realized that his parents took care of him and that he didn't have to worry so much about his family's money (*over-responsibility*). Revising his thinking helped him to set aside some money that he could spend on things for himself.

Test and Change My Thoughts: Oberto

Situation	My Thoughts: What is Going Through My Head?	How Much I Believe Thought 0-100%	Fear Rocket Rating 1-10	Facts That Support Thought / Facts That Don't Support Thought	Revise How Much I Believe Thought 0-100%	What Is A Realistic Way to Think about The Situation?	Revise Fear Rocket Rating 1-10
Picking things up from the ground.	I must pick up these things. **Should**	85%	7	When I pick up things I feel better having them. I'll feel uncomfortable for a little while, but it will go away. My friends don't do this and they're not bothered.	30%	The things I am picking up are not useful; most of these things are trash. I don't have to pick them up.	4
Throwing away things I've collected.	I'll miss having them if I don't. **Overestimating** I like to save the things I have collected. These things want me to have them. **Magical thinking**	95%	9	Keeping my things feels right. Feelings and facts are not the same. These things are not alive. They are inappropriate objects, that's why I hide them.	40%	I can start with small steps to throw the stuff away.	5
Buying things with my own money.	It is important to save money to have for yourself. **Black-and-white thinking**	100%	10	Saving money is a good thing. It's normal to spend some money. I don't need to save all my money because my parents take care of my needs.	50%	I have enough money to buy things as well as save some.	6

Actions to Beat, Control, and Defeat Your Hoarding OCD

Now you can start to use the ABCDs for hoarding OCD. To do this you will need to:

1. **Identify obsessions and compulsions.**
   Use the lists of hoarding obsessions and compulsions to help identify your hoarding behaviors. Identify what it is that you fear. Keep track of your hoarding behaviors, including triggers and feared consequences, for a week using the My Daily Diary worksheet (Appendix).

2. **Rate your behaviors on the Fear Rocket and then list them from high to low.**
   Record your list in the My Obsessions and Compulsions worksheet (Appendix).

3. **Do exposure exercises—fly the fear rocket.**
   Plan exposures. Begin by filling in the diagram to **beat**, **control**, and **defeat** hoarding OCD. Use the actions explained in this chapter and in Chapter 4 to help yourself plan and carry out exposures. Begin your ERP with items lowest on your list.

4. **Change mistaken thoughts about hoarding.**
   Identify mistakes in thinking about hoarding. Use the Test and Change Your Thoughts worksheet (Appendix) to make your thinking more realistic.

How to Beat, Control, and Defeat Hoarding OCD

Use this form to practice the ABCDs of OCD.

1. Write down what the OCD Trickster tells you to worry about.
2. Tell yourself that you know it's the Trickster talking to you trying to scare you.
3. Tell yourself that there is no real reason to be afraid.
4. Tell yourself that you don't have to listen to the Trickster.
5. Tell yourself that you can ride the Fear Rocket safely back down to the ground.
6. Tell yourself that you are getting stronger and the Trickster is getting weaker.

How to Beat, Control, and Defeat Hoarding OCD

Use this form to practice the ABCDs of OCD.

1. Write down what the OCD Trickster tells you to worry about.
2. Tell yourself that you know it's the Trickster talking to you trying to scare you.
3. Tell yourself that there is no real reason to be afraid.
4. Tell yourself that you don't have to listen to the Trickster.
5. Tell yourself that you can ride the Fear Rocket safely back down to the ground.
6. Tell yourself that you are getting stronger and the Trickster is getting weaker.

The Trickster

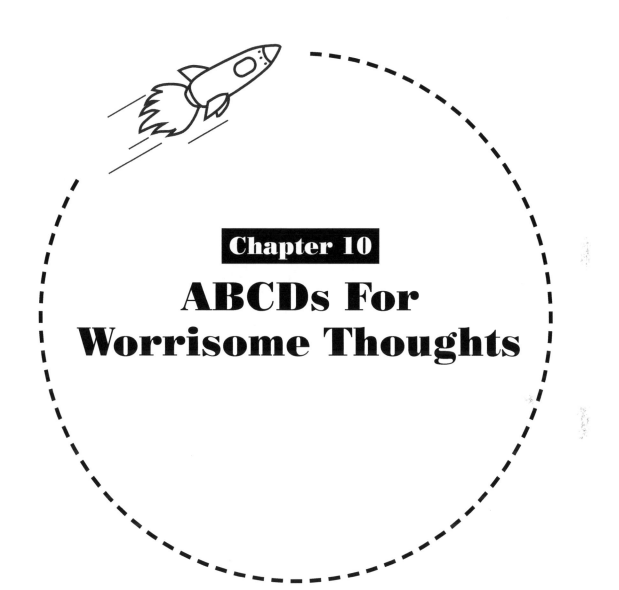

Chapter 10

ABCDs For Worrisome Thoughts

Chapter 10

ABCDs for Worrisome Thoughts

Worrisome thoughts are a problem for many people dealing with obsessive-compulsive symptoms. This chapter can help you to **beat**, **control**, and **defeat** worrisome thought OCD. You will learn about:

- Stories of worrisome thought obsessions and compulsions

- Types of worrisome thoughts

- The worrisome thought vicious circle

- **Actions** to **beat**, **control**, and **defeat** worrisome thought OCD

Stories of Worrisome Thought Obsessions and Compulsions

People with worrisome thought OCD are troubled by unrealistic thoughts about bad things happening. They worry about accidents, injuries, illness, violence, hurting themselves, hurting others, inappropriate sexual conduct, or saying or doing offensive things. They misinterpret the thoughts to mean that they are a bad person for having the thoughts, or they mistakenly believe that the thoughts they have are true, or that they might actually act out the bad thought. None of these things are true. Having bad thoughts does not make them bad people, the thoughts are not true, and they do not act out the bad thought. It is the OCD Trickster making them worry and obsess about the thoughts.

Isaac's Story

Isaac is the boy you learned about in the introduction who says the phrase, "good, better, best," and counts to 10 repeatedly when he has a thought that something bad will happen. Isaac worries a great deal about his father traveling by plane on business trips. Isaac has an unwanted thought that his father's plane will crash and his father will be killed. This is terrifying to Isaac because he believes that having the thought means that it will come true. He uses his special phrase and counting to prevent the plane from crashing. He also pictures his father playing baseball with him as a way of getting rid of the scary image.

Isaac also has fears about something bad happening to his mother. He has images of her being hurt in a car crash. He worries about this every day. Every time that the picture of his mother being killed in a car crash comes into his head he uses his compulsive talking and counting ritual as a way to stop the thought and prevent the accident from happening. His fears about something bad happening to his family have grown worse. The thoughts of his parents being killed or becoming sick are happening often, and Isaac is doing more and more ritualizing to control the worries. He can hardly stand the idea of his father flying. He doesn't want his family to travel by plane or car because of his scary thoughts. He worries that his thoughts could cause the accidents and that he is a bad person for thinking the thoughts.

Lanying's Story

Lanying is a girl who does very well in school, loves soccer and dance, and has lots of friends. She has been bothered recently about doing hurtful things to her friends, her sister, and her parents. She gets thoughts in her head about pushing and kicking her friends. The thoughts seem to come out of the blue. She finds the thoughts to be very upsetting. She is even more upset about thoughts about harming her mother. She thinks that she is going to punch and kick her mother. When the thought comes into her head that she might hurt her mother, she tries to get it out of her head, but the more she tries to get rid of the thought, the harder it is to push it away. She wonders whether she really loves her mother because of having such an awful thought. When she gets the thought, she says, "I love my mother," repeatedly to try to get the thought out of her head.

It is becoming harder and harder for Lanying to stop the violent thoughts. When she even thinks of her mother now she starts worrying. She is very afraid that she will act out on the aggressive thoughts. At school she is also starting to be afraid that she might blurt out something nasty to the teacher. When she thinks this thought she tries to get rid of the worry by picturing a scene in which the teacher and she are both smiling.

Brad's Story

Brad is a boy who has a lot of experience babysitting for his younger sisters and brothers. He really enjoys kids and is saving money from his jobs to buy new gear for ice hockey. He helps his siblings with their homework and figures out ways to entertain them afterward. Brad is a very responsible kid and has a reputation in his neighborhood for being an excellent babysitter. He has become expert at changing babies' diapers, bathing them, and helping them to get to sleep. He gets many compliments from both his parents and neighbors about what a good job he does caring for children. Recently, Brad got very upset when he was taking care of a neighbor's baby. He thought that he may have touched the child's private parts inappropriately when he was changing the diaper. This was a very upsetting thought that made Brad feel very ashamed and embarrassed. He felt so guilty about this that when the neighbors called on Brad to babysit again, he made an excuse about not being available.

He couldn't stop thinking about what he thought had happened, asking himself whether he had purposely touched the baby inappropriately. He goes over this again and again in his mind, trying to reassure himself that he didn't do anything inappropriate. He is also avoiding being alone with his own brothers and sisters. Recently, Brad has also started worrying about touching other kids at school. When he walks down the hall between classes, he tries not to walk too closely to anyone for fear that he could reach out and touch someone.

Types of Worrisome Thoughts

The stories of Isaac, Lanying, and Brad show the types of worrisome thoughts that people have with this type of OCD. The Trickster makes them worry unnecessarily about bad things happening to them or to the people they love and care about. These are terrible and upsetting thoughts. Isaac worries about his parents being hurt or killed; Lanying worries about acting aggressively toward her friends, her mother, and her teacher; and Brad thinks that he touched a child's private parts inappropriately and that he might do it again. The Trickster has fooled them into believing that these terrible things are true. But they are not true. Isaac, Lanying, and Brad have fallen for the lies of the OCD Trickster. People with this type of OCD have to learn that *the thoughts they have are not the problem—it's their response to the thoughts that they need to change*. They have to learn to realize that the thoughts are not true. When they do, they won't have to worry about them anymore.

We know from research on the brain that nearly everyone thinks terrible thoughts sometimes. People without OCD get terrible thoughts just like Isaac's, Lanying's, and Brad's—thoughts about accidents, death, illness, violence, or inappropriate behavior. When people without OCD get these terrible thoughts, they don't pay much attention to them. If they do notice them, they recognize that the thought is not a nice thought, but they know it is not true, and they are able to let the thought go.

People with OCD react very differently to worrisome and terrible thoughts—they fear them—and that's why they get stuck worrying about them.

- They believe the terrible thoughts are true even though they are false.

- They think they are responsible for the terrible thoughts.

- They think they are bad for having the terrible thoughts.

- They try to stop the terrible thoughts by doing a compulsion.

This is what happened to Isaac, Lanying, and Brad. The more they gave in to the Trickster by trying to get rid of the terrible thoughts and worries, the stronger the worries became. When people with OCD react to terrible thoughts this way, it becomes harder to get rid of the thoughts. Understanding the way the brain works helps to explain this.

Try this exercise. Picture a purple camel. Really, really imagine a picture of a purple camel in your head. Make the image as strong as possible. Once you do picture the purple camel, try *not* to think of it *at all* for the next two minutes. Whatever you do, get rid of an image like the purple camel out of your mind.

The people who invented this exercise found that when people try to get rid of the image of the purple camel, they end up thinking about it *more*. That's right! It is the opposite of what you might have predicted. *The more that the people tried to get the picture of the purple camel out of their heads, the more they ended up thinking about it!*

Other people were given opposite instructions. They were told to think *only* about the purple camel and nothing else. *Trying to think only about the purple camel, they thought about the purple camel less!* They ended up thinking about other things. So here's the surprising way that the brain works:

- Try not to think about a thought, try pushing the thought away, and you will end up thinking about it more!

- Try to think about a thought, and only about that thought, and you will end up thinking about it less!

This means that thinking about the terrible thoughts, rather than trying to push them away, is the way to **beat** worrisome thought OCD!

Worrisome Thought Obsessions

The OCD Trickster can make people with OCD worry about many different types of scary and upsetting events. Check out the following list to help identify the types of worrisome thought obsessions that you may be experiencing.

- Worry about people or pets having accidents.

- Worry about people or pets being injured or killed.

- Worry about people or pets getting sick or dying.

- Worry about acting aggressively, harming others, or harming animals.

- Worry about acting out sexually.

- Worry about inappropriate sexual behavior (for example, with children or pets).

- Worry about damaging property.

- Worry about hurting yourself.

- Worry about killing yourself.

- Worry about being gay.

- Worry about saying or doing something inappropriate.

- Worry about loss of control.

- Worry that you don't love or like someone you are supposed to love, or that you hate someone.

- Worry that thinking about something bad will make it happen.

- Worry that thinking bad thoughts makes you bad.

Worrisome Thought Compulsions

There are many different compulsions people do to try to get rid of or control upsetting thoughts. Look at the list below to identify the compulsions that you may be doing.

- Avoiding people, places, or things that make you think about the worrisome thoughts

- Avoiding the thought, trying to stop it, or putting it out of your mind

- Picturing pleasant images or thinking about happy thoughts

- Blocking the thought by using special phrases or numbers

- Washing hands, showering, or cleaning

- Repeating actions a specific number of times

- Performing ritualized actions

- Praying

- Checking or repeatedly going over actions or events to make sure nothing bad happened

- Asking for reassurance

- Repeatedly giving yourself reassurance

- Testing yourself to make sure the worry is not true

- Searching for information that is reassuring

Feared Consequences

People with worrisome thought OCD suffer a great deal because of the bad thoughts. It is difficult for them to realize that the terrible thoughts are not true, that they are not responsible for them, or that they are not bad people because they have the thoughts. People with worrisome thought OCD are actually very good people, that's why they find the thoughts so upsetting. Although the thoughts make them worry that they did, or will do, something bad, people with worrisome thought OCD *do not do the bad things they worry about*. It's the Trickster fooling them into believing this. Identifying what it is that you specifically fear is useful to help you **beat** worrisome thought OCD.

Types of Feared Consequences

- Viewing yourself negatively: seeing yourself as bad, evil, unworthy, defective, unfit, hopeless, or crazy

- Having feelings of guilt: being unable to feel good about yourself, feeling like your life is ruined

- Being viewed negatively by others: being criticized, rejected, abandoned, or seen as bad, evil, or unworthy

- Getting punished: being treated badly, getting sent to jail, losing things or privileges

- Losing control: acting out inappropriate urges

To **beat**, **control**, and **defeat** worrisome thought OCD, you can use the lists of worrisome thought obsessions and compulsions, and feared consequences, to identify your symptoms. To do this, use the My Daily Diary worksheet to keep track of your obsessions and compulsions for a week. Pay attention to what triggers your obsessions and what you think would happen if you don't do a compulsion.

The Worrisome Thought Vicious Circle

Nancy is the girl you learned about in the introduction who worried about being attracted to other girls. The worrisome thought that she might be gay has really interfered with her life. She has isolated herself from friends and avoids watching television shows and going out to certain places because seeing cute girls makes her worry that she is gay. She can't stop worrying about being gay. Nancy is caught in the worrisome thought vicious circle. She has been fooled by the OCD Trickster into worrying about being gay.

Obsessions like Nancy's about her sexual orientation are common among people with worrisome thought OCD. The worry is a form of obsessional doubting. People with this obsession worry that they might be gay and that they won't be able to have a heterosexual relationship. They are really not interested in having a sexual relationship with someone of the same sex, but the Trickster makes them have doubts about it.

Obsessional thoughts about one's sexuality are different from the normal thoughts and worries of gay people. Gay people think of themselves as sexually attracted to people of the same sex. They may or may not worry about the negative attitudes of society toward gay people. Gay people's worries about society's attitudes are different than someone with OCD who has doubts and worries about their sexual orientation. There are gay people with OCD, for example, who may have worrisome thought OCD about whether they are straight!

For people dealing with worrisome thought OCD about being gay, it is important to talk with an OCD expert who can help them understand that their fears about being gay are caused by OCD. Professionals who are not experts on OCD may mistakenly advise people dealing with gay OCD worries that they are in fact gay! As a result, these individuals may not receive the proper cognitive behavioral treatment for their OCD worrisome thoughts.

Nancy got help from a therapist who recognized that she was experiencing gay OCD worries. Nancy's obsessional worry about being gay caused her to do lots of compulsions that made the worry worse. She avoided friends and TV, she avoided looking at magazines with pictures of girls, and she stopped listening to music because it would make her think of the girls dancing in the music videos. She also started to avoid going to places where seeing girls would trigger unwanted thoughts about being gay. When a girl at school who she thought was gay was assigned a seat next to hers in class, she went to class late to avoid sitting next to her. Sometimes she tested herself by deliberately looking at pictures of cute girls to see if she felt attracted to them. She tried to reassure herself that she wasn't gay. She constantly sought reassurance from her mother about being gay. This only made the unwanted thought about being gay occur more.

Exposure Exercises: Flying the Fear Rocket

Nancy worked with the psychologist to **beat** the OCD Trickster. She started by identifying her obsessions, compulsions, triggers, and what she feared would happen if she didn't do her compulsions or compulsive avoidance. She rated each of the behaviors on the Fear Rocket. Her list of obsessions and compulsions can be seen below.

Nancy began flying the Fear Rocket by practicing exposure exercises with items lower on her list. She realized that her compulsive avoidance was making the Trickster stronger and the unwanted worrisome thoughts were getting worse. With repeated practice she knew that could *beat* the Trickster and get *control* over worry about being gay!

Nancy's ERP List of Obsessions and Compulsions

#	Obsessions and Compulsions	Fear Rocket Rating
1	Have a slumber party with girlfriends at my house.	10
2	Sleep over at my girlfriend's house.	9.8
3	Hug and kiss girlfriends when I say hello.	9.6
4	Talk to the girl in class who I think is gay.	9.4
5	Sit next to the girl in class who I think is gay.	9
6	Watch music videos that have sexy girls dancing.	8
7	Watch a movie about girls who are gay.	7.5
8	Do an exposure in which I repeatedly say that I am gay.	7
9	Write a one-paragraph story about a girl coming out.	6.6
10	Read a book in the bookstore café about coming out.	6
11	Read books in the gay and lesbian area of a bookstore.	5.5
12	Watch videos online of girls' coming out stories.	5
13	Walk around the mall and look at girls.	4.5
14	Read online stories about gay celebrities.	4
15	Look at pictures of girls in magazines.	3

Fear Rocket Rating Chart

10 — Going Past The Moon / Panicked
9 — On The Moon / Terrified
8 — Above The Clouds / Scared Stiff
7 — High In The Sky / Very Afraid
6 — Reaching The Sky / Afraid
5 — Getting Higher / Nervous
4 — Going Up / Tense
3 — Taking Off / Uneasy
2 — Firing Up / On Edge
1 — On The Ground / Feeling Calm

Here are the steps Nancy took for practicing ERP on her list of items.

1. Nancy avoided looking at magazines because she was afraid that she would see pictures of girls she thought were cute. The therapist told her that she had to practice avoiding less if she wanted to **beat** the OCD Trickster. She used *self-talk* to do the exposure, saying to herself that she could take her brain back from the Trickster. She said, "I'm not gay, it's the Trickster fooling me into thinking that I am!" She was able to *practice the exposure* by looking at magazines with pictures of cute girls.

2. Next, Nancy looked up stories about gay celebrities online. Reading about these celebrities caused her to worry about being gay because she thought some of them were attractive and that would mean that she could be gay. Again, she used *self-talk* and *encouraged* herself. She said to herself that thinking that celebrities are attractive is ok. Her *mother helped* her as well. Her mother was careful, however, not to give Nancy reassurance. Although more difficult for her, Nancy *repeated these exposures,* flying in the Fear Rocket, until she could look at the celebrities without worry.

3. It was more difficult for Nancy to go to the mall and intentionally look at other girls her age. She used *small steps* to do this exposure. First she went to the mall in the middle of the week at a time when there would be fewer people. She walked around for 10 minutes. She found that her anxiety was not as high as she thought it would be. She *gradually* increased the time she spent walking around the mall. Eventually she was able to go to the mall at times when it was more crowded so that she would see many more girls her own age. For these exposures, she stayed at the mall until her anxiety went down. She did this exposure many times. Now she can go to the mall without worrying.

4. Watching videos online about girls coming out was difficult, but because she had success on the other exercises, Nancy had more confidence about doing this exposure exercise. She did this in steps. With the help of her therapist she looked up girls' coming out videos online. First she watched one with her therapist and then watched it at home with her mother nearby. She talked back to the Trickster, flew the Fear Rocket, and with practice she learned that could watch the coming out videos with no worry.

5. For the next item, reading books in the gay and lesbian area of a bookstore, Nancy did the exposures *gradually*. She went to the local bookstore where she spent time browsing in the gay and lesbian book area. At first she just walked through the area, next she stood at the shelves looking at the books, next she took books off the shelf and stood in the aisle reading for a while. This was a very difficult exposure when other people, especially girls, were standing nearby. She was afraid that they would think she was gay. With lots of *repetition*, this worry went away.

6. Next she sat down in the café area of the bookstore to read one of the books about girls coming out. Finally she purchased a book about girls' coming-out stories. Although her fear was very high at the beginning, doing the exposures in *steps* helped her to fly the Fear Rocket to a safe landing.

7. Nancy practiced the next exposure with the *help of her therapist*. She wrote a one-paragraph story about a girl her own age coming out as gay. The Fear Rocket went up very high for this exposure, but with the help of her therapist, reading the paragraph *repeatedly* made the worry come down. Nancy was getting more and more confident about her ability to **beat** the Trickster.

8. Nancy also worked on the next exposure with her therapist. She *stated her fear to get it out of her head*. She wrote, "I am gay" repeatedly on a piece of paper. This was the most difficult exposure at first. The Fear Rocket went up very high, but with the *encouragement* and *support of her therapist*, she kept saying the fear out loud and her worry lessened with the repetition. *Singing* the words "I am gay" also helped her to fly the Fear Rocket. She worked on this exposure at home as well. She

recorded the phrase on her cell phone voice recorder, saying it over and over for 10 minutes. She *played this back* to herself, sometimes for 40 minutes until the fear went down. This was difficult for Nancy to do. *Writing the obsession, saying it out loud, singing it, recording it, and playing it back* worked to make Nancy's fear go down. She was feeling better and better about her ability to **beat** the OCD Trickster.

9. Nancy felt like she was getting stronger and more confident. Although watching a movie about girls who are gay was scary, Nancy *reminded herself* how successful her efforts had been. She watched the entire movie and then rewatched the most worrisome parts until they didn't bother her anymore. The unwanted and worrisome thought that she might be gay was actually happening less and less.

10. Nancy had avoided watching certain music videos because of her fear that she would see girls dancing who were sexy and cute. She tackled this exposure in *small steps* by first watching these videos during therapy sessions *with her therapist*. She then watched them at home, at first *with her mother*, and then on her own. Once again, the *repeated exposure* made the worry go away so that she wasn't at all worried about seeing the videos.

11. Although afraid to tackle the items highest on her list, Nancy challenged herself by sitting next to the girl in class she avoided because she thought she was gay. She had been going to class late on purpose so that she wasn't able to sit in her usual seat. She was very afraid to do this at first, but all her hard work doing exposure exercises made it easier than she thought it would be.

12. Now that she worried less, talking to her classmate did not turn out to be as hard as she thought. Nancy was glad about this because the girl was a very nice person.

13. Hugging and kissing her girlfriends on the cheek when she greeted them were rated very high on the Fear Rocket. She got ready for this exposure by *rehearsing it in her imagination* and *practicing* it at home *with her mother*. Nancy carried out the real-life exposures in *steps*. She started with hugs for one friend. When she got used to that she added the other friends one at a time. She did the same thing with kissing on the cheek until it really didn't bother her anymore.

14. Feeling more and more confident, she invited one of her girlfriends over her house to study before a test. Originally she hadn't planned on having her friend sleep over, but because she wasn't as worried as she thought, she invited her friend to stay overnight. Nancy was really happy about this, especially because she had felt so bad about not being able to *spend time with her friends.* With the success of having her friend stay over, Nancy accepted an invitation from one of her girlfriends to stay overnight at her house. Although frightened about doing this, she used *self-talk* to encourage herself. Once she got there the worry lessened and she wasn't bothered much by unwanted thoughts.

15. Having all her friends over for a slumber party was the highest item on Nancy's list. She took this exposure on *gradually*. She did many overnights at girlfriends' houses before she felt able to do this. All her hard work was paying off. She was feeling less and less troubled by the obsession and was not really avoiding anything. Having all her friends over felt like a graduation party from behavior therapy—the perfect *reward*!

Changing Fearful Thinking about Worrisome Thoughts

Changing fearful thinking is very useful for **beating** worrisome or terrible thoughts. Nancy did this to help get control of the unwanted thought about being gay. You can see this in the Test and Change Thoughts on page 139. Nancy's worrisome thought that she might be gay became a problem for her because she tried to get rid of the thought and avoid anything that triggered it. That made the doubting worse. Noticing cute girls, something that she did in the past without thinking about it, became evidence that she was gay. When she *tested this thought*, she saw that she was *filtering* the facts to feed her worry. Yes, she did notice cute girls, but she also noticed cute boys. Her girlfriends notice cute girls and they are not gay. These facts led Nancy to *revise her thinking*. She realized that she could notice that a girl is cute without it meaning that she is gay.

Nancy tested and revised the thought that because she worried that she was gay, it must mean that she is gay. Testing this thought, she identified this as the *thought-action fusion* thinking error. This is the mistaken belief that just because you have a thought it must mean that the thought is true. When Nancy tested this thought by *looking at the facts*. She realized that although she noticed girls, she noticed boys as well, she liked the idea of boys liking her, and she liked thinking about going out with boys.

Thinking that she was gay was also an example of *black-and-white thinking*. In her worry about being gay, she *exaggerated* things that she believed meant she was gay and she ignored the facts that showed she wasn't gay. She revised her thinking to be more realistic. She realized that worry about being gay is just in her mind—the facts do not support it.

Test and Change My Thoughts: Nancy

Situation	My Thoughts: What is Going Through My Head?	How Much I Believe Thought 0-100%	Fear Rocket Rating 1-10	Facts That Support Thought / Facts That Don't Support Thought	Revise How Much I Believe Thought 0-100%	What Is A Realistic Way to Think about The Situation?	Revise Fear Rocket Rating 1-10
Looking at girls that are cute.	If I think a girl is cute that means I must be gay. **Filtering**	70%	7	When I see girls, I think that some are cute and others are not. Just saying that someone is cute doesn't mean that you're gay—everyone has opinions about how other people look. My girlfriends make comments about other girls being cute and I don't think that they are gay.	30%	Having an opinion about a girl's looks is normal. I can think someone is cute without wanting to go out with her.	3
Having the thought that I am gay.	If I am worrying about whether I am gay then I must be gay. **Thought-action fusion, Black-and-white thinking**	80%	8	I notice boys who are cute. I like the idea of going out with boys. I have always liked talking about boys with my friends. I like it when boys notice me. Simply having a thought doesn't mean that it's true.	35%	Thoughts about being gay are just thoughts in my imagination. It's the OCD making me doubt myself. The thoughts are not true.	4

Actions to Beat, Control, and Defeat Worrisome Thought OCD

Now you can start to use the ABCDs for worrisome thought OCD.

1. **Identify obsessions and compulsions.**
    Use this chapter's list of worrisome thought obsessions and compulsions to help identify your worrisome thoughts. Identify what it is that you fear. Keep track of your worrisome thoughts, triggers, and feared consequences for a week using the My Daily Diary worksheet (Appendix).

2. **Rate your behaviors on the Fear Rocket and list them from high to low.**
    Record your list in the My List of Obsessions and Compulsions worksheet (Appendix).

3. **Do exposure exercises—Fly the Fear Rocket!**
    Plan exposures. Begin by filling in the diagram to Beat, Control, and Defeat worrisome thought OCD on the next page. Use the actions explained in this chapter and in Chapter 4 to help plan and carry out exposures. Begin your ERP with items lowest on your list.

4. **Change mistaken thoughts about worrisome thoughts.**
    Identify mistakes in thinking. Use the Test and Change Thinking worksheet (Appendix) to make your thinking more realistic.

How to Beat, Control, and
Defeat Worrisome Thought OCD

Use this form to practice the ABCDs of OCD.

1. Write down what the OCD Trickster tells you to worry about.
2. Tell yourself that you know it's the Trickster talking to you trying to scare you.
3. Tell yourself that there is no real reason to be afraid.
4. Tell yourself that you don't have to listen to the Trickster.
5. Tell yourself that you can ride the Fear Rocket safely back down to the ground.
6. Tell yourself that you are getting stronger and the Trickster is getting weaker.

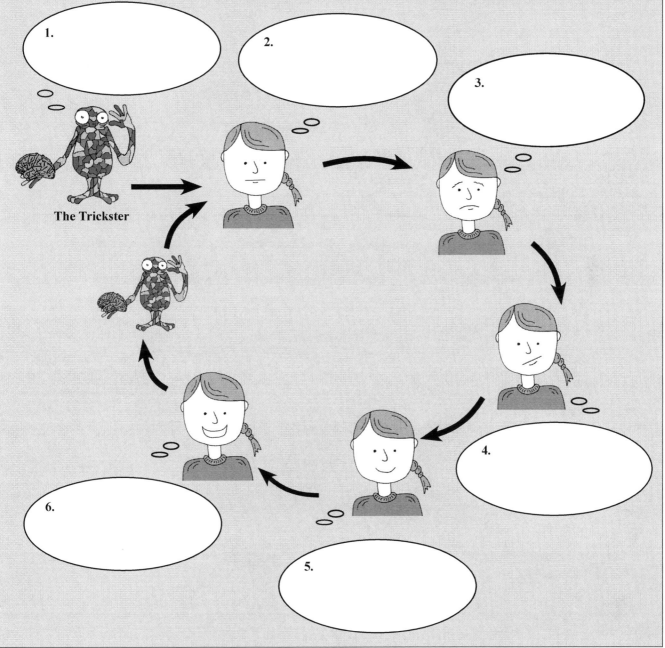

How to Beat, Control, and Defeat Worrisome Thought OCD

Use this form to practice the ABCDs of OCD.

1. Write down what the OCD Trickster tells you to worry about.
2. Tell yourself that you know it's the Trickster talking to you trying to scare you.
3. Tell yourself that there is no real reason to be afraid.
4. Tell yourself that you don't have to listen to the Trickster.
5. Tell yourself that you can ride the Fear Rocket safely back down to the ground.
6. Tell yourself that you are getting stronger and the Trickster is getting weaker.

The Trickster

Chapter 11

ABCDs For Worries about Religion, God, and Sin

Chapter 11

ABCDs for Worries about Religion, God, and Sin

Worries about religion, God, and sin are a problem for many people with OCD. It is called religious OCD. This chapter can help you to **beat**, **control**, and **defeat** religious OCD. You will learn about:

- Stories of religious obsessions and compulsions

- Types of religious OCD

- The religious OCD vicious circle

- **Actions** to **beat**, **control**, and **defeat** religious OCD

Stories of Religious Obsessions and Compulsions

Religious OCD can take a variety of forms. It may occur in people who are not especially religious. Individuals dealing with religious OCD suffer with doubt about the morality of their thoughts and actions, questioning whether what they do, think, feel, or say is moral, immoral, or sinful. They think that they have sinned when they have not. They may be overly concerned about prayer and religious practices, or worry excessively about sin and punishment.

Isabel's Story

Isabel is a girl who worries about being a good person. She thinks that she has to be the best possible person or else she will be punished by God. She has very high standards for herself and worries about being an honest, kind, and charitable person. She saves money from babysitting jobs to donate to poor and homeless people. She is very active in local volunteer organizations. She collects food to donate to the local soup kitchen, and she participates in raising money for the homeless shelter in her town. She signs up for walks/runs to raise money for fights against diseases. She goes around her neighborhood and her school to ask people to make donations to these causes.

Despite all the effort she puts into her volunteering, she doesn't think she is doing enough to help others. She fears that she is disappointing God. She thinks she is failing to do what God wants her to do. Recently she decided that she would give away her dolls and stuffed animals because she thought it was selfish to have them when other people can't afford them. She has also started to cut back on eating. She feels guilty about having so much food when so many people in the world go hungry. Because she has lost weight, her parents have talked to Isabel about the need to eat properly for her health. They also think it is important for Isabel to get help from a therapist. Denying herself food and giving away her belongings is not necessary to being a good person.

Jonah's Story

Jonah is a boy studying at the yeshiva who has problems saying his prayers. He has obsessional doubts about whether he has said them correctly. He doesn't think a prayer is correct unless it is done perfectly and with proper attention. He repeatedly questions whether he has said his prayers correctly or not. He redoes his prayers so much that it is difficult for him to complete ordinary things like eating and going to the bathroom. If he loses his place in a prayer, or has a brief lapse of attention, he gets stuck wondering where he left off. When this happens he feels that he has to go back to the beginning and repeat the prayer. This can happen over, and over, and over. He also has trouble studying. He reads very slowly and rereads to be sure that he has perfect understanding of what he reads. His study partner has to be very patient, because Jonah asks him repeatedly for reassurance about the meaning of what they are reading. Jonah tries the patience of his parents as well. He constantly seeks reassurance about whether he has done or said things correctly. He asks his parents to listen to his prayers to make sure that he has said them the right way.

Jonah has tremendous fear of doing something wrong. This makes it difficult to complete ordinary tasks like getting washed and dressed in the morning. Even getting in and out of cars is difficult because he is so afraid that he could damage a nearby car by opening the car door. He is so careful about this that it takes him a very long time to open and close the door. His obsessions and compulsions have gotten so bad that his parents have sought the help of a rabbi to counsel Jonah about the unrealistic ideas he has about praying and studying.

Abigail's Story

Abigail is a girl who worries a lot about hell and the devil. She thinks that the number 666 is the devil's number, and she tries to avoid looking at, writing, or hearing the number 6 or any number with a 6 in it. The number 9 has also become a problem because she thinks of it as an upside-down 6. She has trouble doing things when the time on the clock has a 6 or a 9 in it. When she has to write a 6 or a 9, she writes down good numbers to counteract the bad ones. If she hears or sees words such as "devil," "hell," or "666," she thinks that she will have bad luck or be harmed. She won't even go out on Halloween because of her fear of the devil. She can't stand the thought of seeing anyone wearing a devil mask or dressing in a devil costume. Not only does she miss out on going trick or treating, she stays in her room to avoid seeing any of the children who come to her house on Halloween. She is terrified that the devil could harm her and that she could go to hell when she dies. Even thinking about the devil or hell scares her. She makes herself feel better by thinking good thoughts or good numbers to counteract the bad ones.

Recently Abigail had unwanted thoughts that she likes the devil and doesn't like God. This is extremely frightening to her. She is now practicing more and more avoidance of trigger situations and has to do more rituals to feel safe from the devil and hell.

Types of Religious OCD

Isabel, Jonah, and Abigail have different forms of religious OCD. They are falling for the lies told to them by the OCD Trickster. Isabel has a version of religious perfectionism. She is trying to live up to extreme and impossible standards for being a good person. It is important to understand the difference between normal standards of morality versus unrealistic OCD standards. People with religious OCD hold to excessively high standards of morality and are overly concerned about being punished if they don't live up to these impossible standards. It is normal to want to be good by being honest, caring, and kind. It is not normal to spend so much time worrying about being good, fearing punishment, or helping others that you don't have time for other things, including fun! It is certainly not normal to stop eating or to give away belongings because of guilt.

Jonah is also dealing with religious perfectionism. He is trying to be perfect in carrying out his prayers and religious practices. Perfectionistic standards about religious practices and rules cause him to pray compulsively. Because of obsessional doubts about whether he has prayed or worshiped properly, his praying is done compulsively. He repeats or redoes prayers until they feel right, he seeks reassurance about whether he has correctly followed religious rules, and he spends too much time worrying about prayers and religious rules. He has fallen behind in his schoolwork, and he has hardly any time for fun stuff like baseball. Normal prayer, worship, and following religious rules does not interfere with other activities like studying, playing, and spending time with family and friends.

Abigail has unrealistic worries about signs and symbols associated with the devil. Her worries that she will be punished for thinking about the devil or for having blasphemous thoughts are similar to worrisome thought OCD. She mistakenly believes that having these thoughts makes her a bad person. The Trickster has fooled Abigail into believing that she can be hurt by objects associated with the devil. She also thinks that she can be punished by God for even thinking these thoughts. These are unrealistic fears. Words, numbers, and symbols cannot harm her. Fears like this are like superstitions or magical thinking.

There are absolutely no facts or evidence to support her fear of numbers, signs, symbols, or words. You could wear a devil mask all day long and it wouldn't have any effect, good or bad, on you—except that people would miss seeing your face!

Obsessions about religion, God, and sin are excessive, unrealistic, and interfere with doing normal activities. The common obsessions and compulsions of religious OCD are show in the lists below.

Obsessions about God, Sin, and Religion

- Overconcern with sin and morality: unrealistic worry about committing a sin, breaking a rule or commandment, or violating the moral code

- Overconcern with inappropriate or embarrassing thoughts or actions: unrealistic worry about asking inappropriate questions, acting impolitely or disrespectfully, or doubting whether one has done so

- Overconcern with religious rituals and practices: unrealistic worry about perfectly observing religious rules, customs of faith, worship, or respecting God or religion

- Overconcern with virtuous behavior: unrealistic worry about goodness, morals, and concern for others

- Superstitious/magical concerns: unrealistic worry about punishment, God, the devil, bad thoughts, impure thoughts, or irreverent thoughts

Compulsions about Religion, God, and Sin

- Avoidance: staying away from persons, places, situations, or things linked to fears (for example, going to church because of fear about praying perfectly)

- Praying or worshiping compulsively: repeating a prayer a certain number of times, or until it feels right, or until it is perfect, or until it is not accompanied by a bad or impure thought

- Repeating: redoing actions, or reviewing or rethinking one's actions, thoughts, or decisions

- Undoing: using good thoughts, numbers, phrases, or actions to neutralize bad thoughts

- Reassurance-seeking: asking others if one has done something properly, completely, or correctly (such as praying)

- Checking for harm: repeatedly making sure that nothing bad has happened such as damage, injury, or a mistake

- Confessing: making repeated or perfect confessions

- Forgiveness-seeking: making sincere or perfect apologies

- Self-denial: depriving oneself of pleasure or nourishment in order to be a good person or as a punishment for an imagined sin or moral failure

- Washing or cleaning: counteracting fears about contact with the devil, bad luck, or evil spirits to decontaminate and prevent harm, punishment, or bad luck

Feared Consequences

People with religious OCD worry unrealistically about whether they have sinned, prayed properly, or are good enough. The main types of feared consequences are shown below.

Types of Feared Consequences

- Punishment by God: being punished for sinning, being disrespectful to God, or for not being good enough

- Being harmed by the devil: worry that the devil will cause bad luck or harm to oneself or loved ones

- Viewing oneself negatively: feeling guilty about failing to live up to the moral code or for causing bad things to happen

- Feeling uncomfortable: being unable to cope with a moral failure

To **beat**, **control**, and **defeat** religious OCD, you can use the lists of religious obsessions and compulsions, and feared consequences, to identify what you have been experiencing. To do this, keep a Daily Diary of your obsessions and compulsions for a week. Pay attention to what triggers your obsessions and what would happen if you don't do the compulsions. To do this, use the My Daily Diary worksheet to keep track of y our obessions and compulsions for a week.

The Religious Vicious Circle

Calvin is the boy we talked about in the introduction who worries about saying his prayers correctly. He says them over and over until he gets them right. He spends a lot of time worrying about whether he did something wrong, sinful, or disrespectful to God. When he goes to church, he never talks except to say prayers and to sing. He tries his best not to look anywhere except at the altar. If anyone says something to him that is not a part of the worship service, he doesn't look at them or answer them because he is afraid that it would be disrespectful to God. If his thoughts drift away from the service for even a brief moment he feels as though he is not behaving respectfully. Even when the service is over he won't talk to anyone after church.

Calvin believes that he has to be extremely careful about sinning. He avoids seeing, hearing, saying, or writing words such as "devil" and "hell" because he thinks they are offensive to God. He feels contaminated when he comes into contact with these words. He has to wash himself and change his clothes in order to protect himself and feel better. He can go through many outfits in a day because of feeling contaminated. He also avoids saying or writing what he considers good words when he feels that his body or his clothing is contaminated. He has a whole list of words that he thinks of as good: "church," "God," "priest," "Jesus," "holy," and "religion." If he thinks of something bad, he says the phrase, "Dear God, please forgive me." He says this compulsive prayer dozens of times throughout the day.

Calvin is caught in the religious OCD vicious circle. He is so worried about offending God that he has even started to avoid going to church because of unrealistic standards about how to act in church. His religious obsessions have gotten so bad that when he comes home from church he has to change his clothes and take a shower. He does this to make sure that he is respectful to God. He doesn't want to come into contact with anything that would be offensive to God. He also spends a long time alone after church. He doesn't want to talk to anyone because he is afraid that this would be disrespectful to God. His parents have asked Calvin to talk to the priest about his fears. Talking to the priest is even difficult for Calvin because of the fear he has about saying or hearing certain words.

Exposure Exercises: Flying the Fear Rocket

Calvin realized that he had to try to beat the religious OCD with behavior therapy. His parents enlisted a therapist and a priest with knowledge of religious OCD to help Calvin. The priest serves as a spiritual advisor to clarify for Calvin and his therapist what are considered normal religious customs and practices.

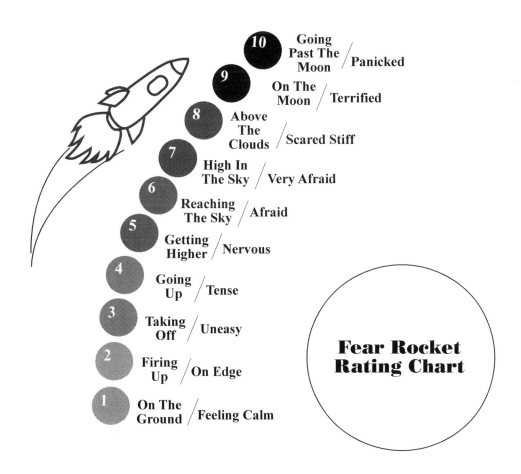

10 — Going Past The Moon / Panicked
9 — On The Moon / Terrified
8 — Above The Clouds / Scared Stiff
7 — High In The Sky / Very Afraid
6 — Reaching The Sky / Afraid
5 — Getting Higher / Nervous
4 — Going Up / Tense
3 — Taking Off / Uneasy
2 — Firing Up / On Edge
1 — On The Ground / Feeling Calm

Fear Rocket Rating Chart

Calvin began by using the My Daily Diary worksheet for a week to help him identify his obsessions, compulsions, triggers, and what he feared would happen if he didn't do the compulsions. The list of his behaviors and ratings on the Fear Rocket are shown below.

Calvin's List of ERP Actions

#	Obsessions and Compulsions	Fear Rocket Rating
1	Do not change clothes or wash after attending church service.	10
2	Answer questions during church service.	9.5
3	Talk on the church grounds after service and on the ride home.	9
4	Unfold hands during church service.	8.5
5	Talk in the car on the way to church service.	8
6	Talk in an empty church when there is no service.	7.5
7	Touch a devil mask without changing clothes.	7
8	Put clothes worn to church into the regular laundry basket.	6.5
9	Talk to others after thinking of words like "devil" and "hell."	6
10	Say and write words considered bad without changing clothes or praying.	6
11	Say and write words like "devil" and "hell" without saying, "Dear God, please forgive me."	5.5
12	Say prayers before bed without repeating them.	5.5
13	Watch religious shows on television without changing my clothes.	5
14	Touch religious objects in my house without changing my clothes.	4
15	Sit in a chair at home considered contaminated because the person sitting in it has used a bad word.	3

Calvin was really tired of worrying all the time about being punished, avoiding normal things, and changing his clothes so much. He began flying the Fear Rocket by *practicing exposures* with lower Fear Rocket ratings.

Here is what Calvin did to beat the OCD.

1. Calvin had been avoiding touching or sitting in a chair at home because a family member who had sat in the chair had talked about heaven, hell, and life after death. Calvin believed that the chair was contaminated as a result. He had been avoiding the chair for months. He even avoided petting the cat if he thought that the cat had been on the chair. Calvin used *small steps* to **beat** the Trickster. First he touched the chair with his hand without washing, then he touched it with both hands, and then he petted the cat sitting in the chair. Next he sat in the chair and *delayed* washing or changing

his clothes. *Gradually* increasing the delay time, Calvin was finally able to sit in the chair without changing his clothes or washing.

2. Next Calvin *practiced* picking up religious objects without washing or changing. He believed that he had to change his clothes after touching them because if he heard, saw, or thought of a bad word while he still had the clothes on it would be sinful and he would be punished. Calvin did the exposure using *small steps*. His *spiritual advisor* explained to Calvin that his fear was not realistic. He wouldn't be punished for normal handling of religious objects. He could touch the religious objects and nothing he encountered after that would cause him to be punished. Although scary to Calvin, he flew the Fear Rocket—and with *repeated practice* stopped the compulsions.

3. Calvin avoided watching any shows on television that dealt with religion, including history shows about religious figures. For this exposure Calvin watched a history show about religious art and *delayed changing* his clothes for an hour. He went on to watch other shows and *delayed* changing his clothes for increasingly longer periods of time. This was a difficult exposure exercise for Calvin, but he eventually *stopped avoiding* watching shows about religious topics because he no longer had to change his clothes.

4. Calvin felt compelled to pray with perfect concentration and respect for God. If he felt it wasn't done correctly he would have to redo the prayers. Sometimes he had to repeat them many times before he felt they were correct. This was a very frustrating situation for Calvin because he could end up going to bed very late. He *talked this over with his spiritual advisor* and *rehearsed the exposure* with him. His spiritual advisor showed Calvin that it's okay to make a mistake when he prays and that he doesn't have to go back to redo the prayer if he loses concentration. He also *rehearsed the exposure with his therapist*. Having *prepared himself* so well, he was able to *reduce* the number of times he repeated his prayers (*small steps*), at first limiting the repetitions to no more than three, then two, and then to no repetitions at all.

5. It was equally difficult for Calvin to say and write words like "devil" and "hell" without a compulsive prayer to God asking for forgiveness. This exposure was carried out in a series of *steps*. He started by saying words that were less scary, beginning with a name like "Michelle" with the word "hell" in it. Calvin *repeatedly wrote and said* this word until it didn't scare him anymore. He did the same thing with words that were harder for him to say or write. Sometimes if a word was particularly difficult, he *sang* it first or *made up a song* with the word in it. This helped him to worry less about being punished for saying the words. Eventually he stopped the compulsive praying.

6. Once Calvin had eliminated compulsively praying after saying and writing the words, he moved on to eliminating the compulsion about changing his clothes after saying the words. At first he *postponed* changing his clothes for a half hour after *saying and writing the words*, and he kept increasing this 15 minutes at a time. He *repeated this practice*, sometimes *singing the words*, and *making up songs* to ride the Fear Rocket through the worry. He kept extending the time he waited to change until he didn't have to change clothes at all.

7. Calvin avoided talking to anyone if he thought of words that he believed were scary, like "hell," "devil," "sin," and "evil." He refused to talk until he was able to perform his decontaminating compulsions. He was afraid that he would be responsible for causing harm to another person by speaking to him or her while he felt contaminated. He *talked with his spiritual advisor* about this fear and then *rehearsed* saying the words out loud *with his therapist*. He then *practiced* doing this exposure at home *with his parents*. This was a very difficult exposure for Calvin and required *lots of practice* flying the Fear Rocket. It did eventually get easier, and he was able to talk normally even after thinking about the words.

8. Calvin never wore the clothes he wore to church anywhere else. Clothes worn to church were kept in a separate laundry basket and washed separately from the rest of his clothes. Calvin took on this exposure on by using *small steps.* He began by putting one piece of clothing worn to church into the regular laundry basket, then two, then three, and so on. *Little by little* he stopped compulsively separating the clothes worn to church. He no longer thought of certain clothes as special and could wear any of his clothes anywhere at any time, including the shoes that he usually wore only to church.

9. Touching the devil mask without changing clothes was done *gradually.* He was afraid of touching the mask because of fear of God's punishment. He received *support* for this exposure *from both the priest and his therapist.* He touched the mask with only one finger at first, then two, three, four, and five (*small steps*). Then he did it with both hands. He also *delayed* washing and changing his clothes after touching the mask. With lots of *hard work and repetition,* Calvin was able to touch the devil mask without worry.

10. Calvin was very afraid of talking in church because of his obsession that God would punish him for being disrespectful. He refused to talk in the car riding to and from church and stayed in his room for more than an hour after church to avoid talking with others. These exposures were rated very high on the Fear Rocket. Calvin received *support from his spiritual advisor* who helped him to understand that his *fears were very unrealistic.* First he carried out the exposure by going to church with his therapist to *practice talking* in the parking lot (*small steps*). After doing this several times, Calvin went inside the church with his therapist. They sat in a pew and talked to one another. Calvin *repeated this exposure* until his worry about punishment went away.

11. For the next exposure—talking with his family in the car on the way to Sunday services—Calvin *rehearsed this exposure with his therapist.* Next Calvin *practiced* by driving to church *with his parents on weekdays (small steps).* After this *preparation,* Calvin agreed to talk in the car on the way to church by answering one question the first week. Once he accomplished this, he increased his talking week by week until he could talk normally on the way to church.

12. Calvin built on this successful exposure by *practicing* unfolding his hands during the church service *a little at a time.* Once again he did this in *steps* after *rehearsing this with his therapist.* At first he unfolded his hands for a minute before the service began. He then *practiced* doing this for a minute during the actual service, extending the time until he could sit in the pew without folding his hands at all.

13. Talking after the church service on the church grounds and on the ride home in the car was an even more difficult exposure for Calvin. He began by talking this over with his *spiritual advisor* and *rehearsing* it with his therapist. Taking *small steps,* Calvin started by answering only one question the first week and then increasing the amount he talked *a little more* each week until he could talk normally.

14. Calvin followed the same *small steps* to do the exposure of talking during church services. Just as Calvin had refused to unfold his hands during church services, he refused to talk during services if it wasn't an official prayer. To begin, Calvin talked this over with his *spiritual advisor* and *rehearsed talking with his therapist* in the church when there was no service being conducted. On the day Calvin agreed to do an actual exposure, he answered one question asked by his parents. Each week Calvin practiced giving brief answers to questions, flying the Fear Rocket until he worried no more about politely talking in church.

15. After working on all his exposure exercises, Calvin was ready to tackle the highest item on his list. After going to church, Calvin would usually come home and immediately change his clothes and wash. He did this because he thought it would be sinful for him to come in contact with any words he thought of as bad while dressed in clothes worn to church. The Trickster made this a very difficult exposure exercise for Calvin. He managed to fly the Fear Rocket through the worry with the *encouragement of his spiritual advisor*. He also *rehearsed* doing this with his *therapist* and in his *imagination*. Calvin succeeded and felt really happy about **beating**, **controlling**, and **defeating** the OCD!

Changing Fearful Thinking about Religious OCD

Calvin worked on changing his fearful thinking to help with the exposure exercises. The worksheet on the next page shows how Calvin tested and revised his unrealistic thinking about prayer, sin, and God. Calvin refused to talk to others if he was thinking about a word he considered bad because he feared that he would spread harmful contamination to others. When he looked at the facts that supported this thought he said that bad words could be a sign of disrespect. No facts supported his belief that words or numbers hurt people by contaminating them. This belief is an example of superstitious or magical thinking. Saying words or numbers cannot cause harmful effects through contamination. Words are just words, numbers are just numbers. In fact, the fear of the number 666 is nothing more than a superstition. As Calvin's spiritual advisor explained to him, the number 666 has nothing to do with the devil. It was used in the Bible as a symbol for Nero, the Roman emperor. *Testing and revising* his thinking led Calvin to be less afraid of words and numbers.

Calvin *tested and revised* the thought that he should separate the clothes he wore to church from all his other clothes. This thinking is an example of a *should mistake in thinking*—exaggerating the need to be respectful of God by taking special care of clothes. Calvin's spiritual advisor explained to Calvin that separating clothes doesn't have anything to do with respecting God. His thinking about the clothes is an example of *magical or superstitious thinking* that clothes worn to church could be contaminated by other clothes. Clothes are the same wherever they are not usually worn. None are contaminated.

Calvin's belief that talking before, during, or after church is disrespectful to God is also an example of a *should* thinking mistake. When he looked at the facts that support this belief, he said that he had been taught by his teachers and parents not to talk in church. Calvin took this to mean that he should never talk in church. If he talked even once, he believed that it would be disrespectful to God—an example of *black-and-white thinking*. Calvin's spiritual advisor explained to him that polite and brief talking in church is acceptable. The facts also did not support his mistaken idea that he would be punished if he talked in church—an example of *overestimating*—exaggerating the likelihood of being punished. He tested this belief by looking at other people who he knew talked in church, including his parents, who were never punished for talking. Based on the facts, he revised his thinking to be more realistic. He realized that it was okay to talk in church at times as long as you did so quietly and did not bother others.

Trigger	My Thoughts - What is Going Through My Head	How Much I Believe Thought 0-100%	Fear Rocket Rating 1-10	Facts That Support Thought / Facts That Don't Support Thought	Revise How Much I Believe Thought 0-100%	What Is A Realistic Way to Think about The Situation?	Revise Fear Rocket Rating 1-10
Talking to others after thinking words like "devil" and "hell."	I will cause other people harm by spreading the contamination from bad words. **Magical Thinking**	65%	6	Bad words are a sign of disrespect. Words alone can't hurt people. Other people use these words and don't worry about being punished or causing harm to others.	30%	Words are different than actions. I can say a word that is bad or good without it causing anything to happen.	3
Putting clothes worn to church into the laundry.	These clothes should not be treated disrespectfully. **Shoulds, Magical Thinking**	70%	6.5	I have been taught to respect God. The priest said this doesn't have anything to do with respect for God.	35%	Clothes worn to church are like other clothes and don't have to be separated.	3
Talking before, during, or after church.	Talking like this is disrespectful to God. I'll be punished. **Shoulds, Overestimating, Black-and-white thinking**	80%	9.5	Sunday-school teachers and my parents told us not to talk in church. The priest said that polite and brief talking in church is appropriate. Other people I respect talk occasionally in church and nothing bad happens.	40%	As long as I talk quietly and don't bother others, answering or asking appropriate questions is okay to do. It is not disrespectful.	4

Actions to Beat, Control, and Defeat Religious OCD

Now you can start to use the ABCDs for religious OCD.

1. **Identify obsessions and compulsions.**
   Use this chapter's lists of obsessions and compulsions about religion, God, and sin to help identify your religious obsessions and compulsions. Identify what it is that you fear. Keep track of your obsessions, compulsions, triggers, and feared consequences for a week using the My Daily Diary worksheet (Appendix).

2. **Rate your behaviors on the Fear Rocket and list them from high to low.**
   Record your list in the My Obsessions and Compulsions worksheet (Appendix).

3. **Do Exposure Exercises—Fly the Fear Rocket!**
   Plan exposures. Begin by filling in the diagram to Beat, Control, and Defeat Religious OCD on page 157. Use the actions explained in this chapter and Chapter 4 to help plan and carry out exposures. Begin your ERP with items lowest on your list.

4. **Change mistaken thoughts about religious OCD.**
   Identify mistakes in thinking about God, sin, and religion. Use the tools in Chapter 5 and the Test and Change Your Thoughts worksheet (Appendix) to make your thinking more realistic.

How to Beat, Control, and Defeat Religious OCD

Use this form to practice the ABCDs of OCD.

1. Write down what the OCD Trickster tells you to worry about.
2. Tell yourself that you know it's the Trickster talking to you trying to scare you.
3. Tell yourself that there is no real reason to be afraid.
4. Tell yourself that you don't have to listen to the Trickster.
5. Tell yourself that you can ride the Fear Rocket safely back down to the ground.
6. Tell yourself that you are getting stronger and the Trickster is getting weaker.

Worksheet

How to Beat, Control, and
Defeat Religious OCD

Use this form to practice the ABCDs of OCD.

1. Write down what the OCD Trickster tells you to worry about.
2. Tell yourself that you know it's the Trickster talking to you trying to scare you.
3. Tell yourself that there is no real reason to be afraid.
4. Tell yourself that you don't have to listen to the Trickster.
5. Tell yourself that you can ride the Fear Rocket safely back down to the ground.
6. Tell yourself that you are getting stronger and the Trickster is getting weaker.

Chapter 12

Working on Scary Obsessions and Compulsions

Working on Scary Obsessions and Compulsions

You've come a long way since starting to learn the **actions** to **beat**, **control**, and **defeat** OCD. It's good to look back to see how far you have come. Have the Fear Rocket ratings gone down? Are you still doing any of the compulsions? Are you avoiding any situations because of OCD? Have you reached the items that are highest on your list of obsessions and compulsions, and are you finding it difficult to do the exposures? If so, don't give up now. You are like the mountain climber who has nearly made it to the top. It may be a steep climb, but once you take a breather and plan a good route, you can successfully climb the rest of the way up. It is worth the effort to continue using **actions** to **beat**, **control**, and **defeat** OCD. This chapter will help you to work on tackling the items that you rated high on the Fear Rocket. You will learn about:

- Coping with scary obsessions and compulsions

- Small-step exposure plans

- Action experiments

Coping with Scary Obsessions and Compulsions

Gemal is the boy with contamination obsessions and compulsions about bad luck rubbing off on him from contact with some of his classmates. He practices lots of avoidance because of his OCD worries. When he does come into contact with people, places, or things that he thinks are contaminated, he has to wash himself and his things. He takes very long showers and stores or throws his things away because of his contamination fears. Gemal worked on his list of obsessions and compulsions by doing exposure and response prevention exercises. He started by practicing exposures with the items rated lowest on the Fear Rocket and worked his way up to the higher-rated items. When he got to the highest items, his progress slowed down. You can see Gemal's list of obsessive compulsive items on the next page. Flying the Fear Rocket became difficult for him when he reached item #13.

Gemal's ERP list of Obsessions and Compulsions

#	Obsessions and Compulsions	Fear Rocket Rating
1	Reduce shower time at night, then recontaminate.	10
2	Unpack and use stored items considered contaminated.	9.5
3	Buy and eat ice cream in the store where kids who I consider to be contaminated work.	9
4	Reduce hand washing to end on a number considered bad.	8.5
5	Add names of kids considered contaminated as friends to my page on the website.	8
6	Go online to look at messages and photos, and to chat with friends.	7.5
7	Delay washing after school.	7
8	Listen to my parents say the names of kids considered contaminated.	6.5
9	Wear a sweatshirt with the school name and logo.	6
10	Watch the local news that mentions my town and school.	5.5
11	Look at the local newspaper.	5
12	Use my cell phone in school without washing it later at home.	4.5
13	Look at pictures of classmates considered contaminated without washing hands.	4
14	Use schoolbooks at home without washing them.	3.5
15	Look at a picture of school without washing my hands.	3

10 — Going Past The Moon / Panicked
9 — On The Moon / Terrified
8 — Above The Clouds / Scared Stiff
7 — High In The Sky / Very Afraid
6 — Reaching The Sky / Afraid
5 — Getting Higher / Nervous
4 — Going Up / Tense
3 — Taking Off / Uneasy
2 — Firing Up / On Edge
1 — On The Ground / Feeling Calm

Fear Rocket Rating Chart

Small-Steps Exposure Plans

Gemal was too afraid to do exposures with the highest items on his list. But Gemal did not give up. He talked with his therapist and parents to figure out a way for him to tackle the highest items. He created a detailed Small-Step Exposure Plan for each of the top items. You can see the step-by-step plan he devised for item #13 that you will see next.

Gemal's Small-Step Exposure Plan for #13

Step	Buy and eat ice cream in the store where kids who I consider to be contaminated work.	Fear Rocket Rating
1	Buy and eat an ice cream cone in the shop in town where the contaminated kids work.	9
2	Eat a small sample of ice cream handed to me by the kids working behind the counter.	8
3	Walk into the ice cream shop and talk to the kids working behind the counter.	7
4	Walk past the ice cream shop where the contaminated kids work.	6
5	Eat a spoonful of ice cream. Don't wash afterward.	5
6	Scoop out ice cream from the container purchased in the store where the contaminated kids work. Don't wash afterward.	4

Carrying out the exposures in this *step-by-step* fashion enabled Gemal to tackle this tough exposure. The Small-Step Exposure Plan is an organized way of using the *small steps* technique to carry out exposure exercises. His plan included six steps, but the number of steps you use is up to you. You can put in as many as you need for carrying out exposures with difficult items. The example on the next page shows eight steps in the Small-Step Exposure Plan for item #14 on Gemal's list.

Gemal's fears about bad luck started when the Trickster made him afraid of kids in school he thought had problems. These were kids that he saw as less fortunate than him because they did poorly in school, came from poor families, were disliked by others, or were not good athletes. He feared that contact with them would cause him to have the same problem. He became so fearful of these kids that he actually stopped going to school for a period of time. He thought that all of his belongings from that difficult time—clothes, binders, books, backpack—were contaminated. Because he wouldn't touch any of his things, much less wear the clothes, his parents stored them in boxes that were put into the garage. Gemal wouldn't go near them. To help himself to reduce the compulsive avoidance, he devised the Small-Step Exposure Plan that you see below.

Gemal's Small-Step Exposure Plan for #14

Step	Unpack and use stored items considered contaminated.	Fear Rocket Rating
1	Use my belongings and wear clothes without washing afterward.	9.5
2	Put the clothes away in my drawers and closet without washing afterward.	8.5
3	Unpack the clothes from the box without washing afterward.	8
4	Put the books on the bookshelf in my room without washing afterward.	7.5
5	Unpack the rest of the books without washing afterward.	7
6	Unpack one book from one box without washing afterward.	6
7	Bring boxes from garage into the house without washing afterward.	5
8	Touch the outside of boxes considered contaminated without washing afterward.	4

The item at the top of Gemal's list, reducing his nighttime showering and then recontaminating, was the scariest one for Gemal to tackle. He worked on reducing his shower time with only partial success. He could do a lot of exposures during the day, including going to school, as long as he was able to take a shower at night to decontaminate himself. Depending on how contaminated he felt, these showers could last up to two hours. Gemal washed himself repeatedly so that he ended on a good number. The Small-Step Exposure Plan he devised to help him reduce his showering and then to be able to recontaminate afterward is shown in the chart below.

Gemal's Small-Step Exposure Plan for #15

Step	Reduce shower time at night, then recontaminate.	Fear Rocket Rating
1	Take a 15-minute shower then recontaminate.	10
2	Take a 20-minute shower then recontaminate.	9.5
3	Take a 30-minute shower then recontaminate.	9
4	Take a 45-minute shower then recontaminate.	8
5	Take a 60-minute shower then recontaminate.	7
6	Take a 75-minute shower.	6
7	Take a 1½-hour shower.	5
8	Take a 1¾-hour shower.	4

Gemal reduced the number of times he washed himself in order to cut down the time he spent in the shower. He practiced reducing his shower time until he got it down to 15 minutes. This took enormous courage, hard work, and time for Gemal to accomplish, but he did it and moved on to the higher items on his list involving showering less and recontaminating after his shower.

After Gemal showered at night he would be careful not to become contaminated again. He stayed in his room, didn't go on the Internet, and didn't watch TV. It was very difficult for him to tackle the exposure of recontaminating after his shower. In the beginning, he did this by just *picturing images* of contaminated kids in his head. Next he *said their names out loud*. Next he *wrote them down*. Next he went online, chatted with friends, and looked at pictures of contaminated kids. He used *small steps* in to do the recontamination exposures. It worked! Gemal **beat**, **controlled**, and **defeated** OCD! You can use the worksheets on page 165 to devise a Small-Step Exposure Plan.

Action Experiments

Gemal worked on *changing his thinking* to be more realistic by setting up an Action Experiment. You learned about this technique in Chapter 4. It is a useful action for changing thinking errors. Gemal predicted that he could get bad luck from contact with some of his classmates (*overestimating, magical thinking*, and *thought-action confusion*). The specific consequences of contamination that he feared were:

- He would be rejected by his friends.

- He would do poorly in school, maybe even fail.

- His personality would change so that he wouldn't be himself.

- He would do poorly in sports.

- His family would be harmed (for example, his parents would divorce).

Gemal set up an Action Experiment to test his predictions. He did this by eating a spoonful of ice cream brought home from the shop where the *contaminated* kids worked. He did this every day for a week. He also ate the ice cream after he took his shower at night when he would usually avoid touching anything that he thought was contaminated.

For a week before he carried out the Action Experiment—and on each day of the experiment—Gemal used the My Daily Diary worksheet to record how his day went. He recorded what happened to him and whether it was good, bad, or neutral. By using the My Daily Diary, Gemal collected information about whether eating the ice cream was as dangerous as he predicted it would be. The chart below shows how Gemal carried out the experiment. Most important, the results of the Action Experiment helped him to change his thinking. He understood that eating the ice cream handled by the contaminated kids was not really a threat to him or his family.

Gemal's Action Experiment

Steps for *Action Experiment*	Gemal's Experiment
Prediction: What exactly do I think will happen?	When I eat ice cream from the shop where contaminated kids work, I will have bad luck.
Rate how much I believe it.	I believe this will happen 100%.
Experiment that tests the prediction.	Eat a spoonful of ice cream after showering.
Get a helper to assist doing the experiment.	Mom brought home ice cream purchased from the shop where contaminated kids work.
Carry out the experiment.	Eat a spoonful of ice cream.
Record the results.	Did not have bad luck.
Revise the belief in my thought.	Belief that I will have bad luck is 10%.
Revise my thought.	Nothing bad will happen from eating ice cream handled by contaminated kids. Bad things can happen, but it is not due to eating ice cream!

You can do Action Experiments just like Gemal did to help with your exposure exercises. He set up several Action Experiments to assist working on the scary exposures. Another way to gather information for an Action Experiment is to survey other people about their experiences. Gemal asked classmates about their experiences with the kids he believed to be contaminated. He also collected information from his experiences prior to developing his obsession about bad luck. He asked himself how often negative things occurred when he came into contact with the kids. He asked how often negative things did not occur.

Information collected from others and yourself can help you to think more realistically. It helps you to not see risk when there is none. Very important, it can help you fly in the Fear Rocket for scary exposure actions. You can use the worksheet on page 165 to record your Action Experiment.

Although it may be difficult to do, tackling the scary obsessions and compulsions is really important. If you don't **beat** them back, the Trickster will hang on to your brain and try to grab hold of more. So even if your progress is slow and your gains seem small, keep up your exposures. It may take a while, but *small steps* will get you to the top of the mountain! As you carry out your exposure exercises, remember that you can use the change you learned in Chapters 2, 3, 4 and 5. **Do the exposures every day and often. Say to yourself, "I can beat the OCD Trickster!"** Remember that the more you fly the Fear Rocket to a safe landing, the easier it becomes. Repetition wins the day! You get stronger and the Trickster gets weaker.

Actions to Beat, Control, and Defeat Scary Obsessions & Compulsions

1. Devise Small-Step Exposure Plans.

2. Write a list of small exposures and rate them on the Fear Rocket. List the items from high to low.

3. Do exposure actions—fly the fear rocket!

4. Plan and carry out Action Experiments.

Small-Step Exposure Plan

#	Small-Step Exposure Plan Item #	Fear Rocket Rating

Action Experiment

Steps for *Action Experiment*	*My Action Experiment*
Prediction: What exactly do I think will happen?	
Rate how much I believe it: 0-100%	
Experiment that tests the prediction.	
Get a helper to assist doing the experiment.	
Carry out the experiment.	
Record the results.	
Revise the belief in my thought.	
Revise my thought.	

Chapter 13

After You Beat, Control and Defeat OCD

After You Beat, Control, and Defeat OCD

Keeping Up Your Good Actions

OCD FEAR ROCKET

You have done it! You have learned to use **actions** to **beat**, **control**, and **defeat** the OCD Trickster! You are now an experienced Fear Rocket flyer! By flying the Fear Rocket you have become stronger and more powerful than the OCD Trickster! You are now an experienced Fear Rocket pilot! You can fly the Fear Rocket from high in the sky to a safe and controlled landing. It's time to congratulate yourself! You deserve lots of credit for your bravery, hard work, and dedication in standing up to the OCD Trickster. There you are standing tall! Be proud of yourself!

The Trickster Is Small and Weak

Congratulations!

Check Out Your Progress

Now it is time to see how much progress you have made. In Chapter 3, "The ABCDs to Beat OCD," you learned how to identify obsessions and compulsions and use the My Daily Diary worksheet to help you do that. Look back at your list of obsessions and compulsions. Look at the Fear Rocket ratings you gave each of the items. Now take a moment to rerate each of the items. How much have the Fear Rocket ratings gone down? Have you improved your ability to resist doing compulsions? Are you able to fly the Fear Rocket down from the sky? Are you less afraid about not doing a compulsion? Are any items on your list rated 4 or higher? If so, then *don't stop working on your list*. Keep doing exposures until the obsessions don't bother you anymore and your Fear Rocket ratings are 0 or 1. If you are finding it difficult to tackle items rated high on the Fear Rocket, read Chapter 12 for tips on doing exposures for particularly scary obsessions and compulsions. Whatever you do, keep flying the Fear Rocket until you **beat**, **control**, and **defeat** the Trickster.

Keeping Up Your ABCDs

The ABCDs you have learned are **actions** for life. You need to practice them so that you stay stronger and more powerful than the OCD Trickster. Good athletes practice to stay physically fit and succeed in their sports. Whatever the sport—soccer, baseball, football, tennis, hockey, softball, skating, track and field, running, wrestling, or bicycle racing—athletes *train and practice* to stay strong and fit. You must do the same thing to **beat** back, **beat** up, **control**, and **defeat** the Trickster. You need to be mentally fit!

The Trickster will try to push you around again. It will try to fool you into worrying about something that is not true. It will try to get you to do a compulsion to feel better. By practicing all the actions you have learned, you will be ready to **beat** the Trickster. Review the **actions** you have learned. Do this *once a week* for the next month. After that, review the **actions** at least *once a month*.

Holding on to everything you have learned will help you to **beat** back the Trickster when it tries to grab hold of your brain again. This means that you need to pay attention to the things that trigger your obsessions—the people, places, things, thoughts, and situations that you identified in your OCD Daily Diary. Don't avoid your trigger situations. Go out of your way to expose yourself to them so that you can practice your exposure skills and fly the Fear Rocket. If you find yourself doing any kind of compulsion, or some version of an old compulsion, remind yourself to fly the Fear Rocket. Look at it as an opportunity to practice your exposure skills. The more you expose yourself to the scary things without giving in to the Trickster, the stronger you will be.

Understanding OCD: Review Chapter 2

Go back to Chapter 2 to review the understanding you have of how OCD works. Practicing this is important because it keeps you on your guard. You have to watch out for the Trickster so that you will be ready to **beat** it back as soon as it tries to fake you out. When it tries to grab hold of your brain, the first thing to do is to say, "It's the Trickster trying to fool me! I don't have to listen to it." Use your skills so that you don't get stuck in the OCD vicious circle. When the Trickster makes you worried, bravely fly the Fear Rocket through the clouds of worry and fear! You know how to do it and you can do it again. This is how you **beat**, **control**, and **defeat** OCD.

The ABCDs to Beat OCD: Review Chapter 3

Exposure and response prevention (ERP) is the main **action** to use to **beat** OCD. Standing up to the Trickster means that you need to identify your obsessions and compulsions. What is the Trickster telling you to worry about? What does it tell you to do or to avoid? What do you do to make yourself feel better? The Trickster has lots of tricks up its sleeves to fool you into worrying. It is important to recognize them as tricks—fake worries and fears. Review the lists of obsessions and compulsions to help you recognize them. Also reread the chapter that deals with your specific type of OCD, Chapters 6 to 11.

ABCDs of Coping with Fear: Review Chapter 4

Practicing ERP will keep you stronger and more powerful than the OCD Trickster. Repeatedly riding the Fear Rocket through the worry and fear to a safe landing will help you to **beat**, **control**, and **defeat** the OCD Trickster. It is really important to keep your ERP skills sharp so that you can use them when you need them. Be sure to review Chapter 4 for all the different ways you can carry out ERP against OCD. Understanding fear and how to manage it helps you to cope with OCD as well as the normal stress that occurs in life. Managing fear is really a life skill.

ABCDs of Fearful Thinking: Review Chapter 5

How you think determines what you feel and what you do. What you say to yourself can help you to **beat** back the OCD Trickster. Paying attention to what you say to yourself is a skill that you can practice every day. When you feel any negative feeling—fear, worry, anger, guilt, or sadness—stop for a moment to ask what you are saying to yourself. What thoughts are making you feel that way? Identify the thinking errors in what you are saying. Test and revise your thoughts to be more realistic. Changing your thinking to be more realistic can help you beat the OCD Trickster. Review all the actions that help you to think more realistically. Turn to Chapter 4 for a refresher. These actions can help you **beat** OCD. Practicing thinking realistically is also a life skill for coping with the ups and downs of life.

Working on Scary Obsessions and Compulsions: Review Chapter 12

At some point the Trickster may frighten you with an especially scary obsession. You will be blasted high into the sky on the Fear Rocket. You will find it difficult not to do the compulsion because you want fast relief from the fear. When this happens, remind yourself that you are an experienced, accomplished, and successful Fear Rocket flyer. *Don't jump out!* By staying in the Fear Rocket you can fly safely down and away from the OCD Trickster. By resisting the compulsion it may take longer for the fear to decrease, but the more you do it the easier it will get. Reread Chapter 4 for tips. You won't get caught in the OCD vicious circle. You will fly with confidence through clouds of fear and worry.

OCD FEAR ROCKET

When you are faced with scary obsessions and compulsions, you can use your exposure tools to **beat** the Trickster. Remember to use *self-talk* to *encourage* yourself. Remind yourself that it's the Trickster trying to fool you and that you don't have to listen to it. Figure out a Small-Step Exposure Plan and carry it out. Remind yourself that *small steps* still get you to the goal. Design Action Experiments to help you change your thinking to be more realistic. Review the checklist of Exposure and Response Prevention actions to figure out ways to help you beat the Trickster.

What Happens When the Trickster Comes Back

OCD symptoms come and go in people's lives. Sneaky thing that it is, the Trickster won't give up trying to fool you into worrying and doing unneeded compulsions. Even when you have successfully completed exposures for all the items on your list, or new obsessions can pop up to bother you. That's why it is so important to keep practicing your skills.

Knowing that the Trickster will come back does not have to be a big problem. What is likely to happen is that an old obsession will creep in, at first you may not notice it, but you may find yourself doing an old compulsion or a lesser version of it. For example, Nancy is the girl who had an obsessional worry that she might be gay. Nancy got her OCD under control by doing *exposure exercises* and *changing her fearful thinking*. Recently the thought went through her head that she is attracted to cute girls. She found herself looking away from girls when this happened. Then she tried to test herself by looking at them on purpose to see if she felt attracted to them (compulsive *reassurance seeking*).

It took some time for Nancy to realize that it was the Trickster trying to fool her again. When she did, she stopped herself from falling back into her old responses to the Trickster. Instead she used her exposure tools. She wrote down, "I am gay. I am attracted to girls." She *wrote it out* 100 times. She *recorded it* and listened to it over and over. She *sang it* repeatedly. Exposing herself to the scary thought in these ways made it go away. She also worked on changing her unrealistic thinking about being gay by *examining the facts*. Nancy succeeded in **beating**, **controlling**, and **defeating** the OCD once again. It was easier to do this time because of her success before.

What Nancy did is what you have to do when the Trickster tries to bother you again. Don't fall back into doing your old or new compulsions. **Beat** back the OCD Trickster right away. Talk to yourself. Tell yourself it's the Trickster trying to fool you again. Remind yourself that you **beat** it before and you can do it again. Use your understanding of OCD to plan and carry out exposures. Work on changing your unrealistic thinking.

Regaining Gains

What if you fall back into doing some of your old compulsions or start new ones? Maybe you are finding it hard to fly the Fear Rocket. Perhaps you feel like you are going backward, losing some of your gains. Again, it is not a big deal. Everyone experiences obstacles that block their progress. Setbacks are part of life. Athletes go into slumps, they are injured, their equipment breaks, they get tired, they lose motivation, their skills need sharpening, or they come up against a more powerful opponent. Do good players give up? They do not. They try harder. They may have to come from behind, but they keep trying. And don't forget that losing some of your gains doesn't put you all the way back where you started. You simply have a few steps to retrace. A hiker who goes off the trail for a bit returns to the trail where he or she left it to continue the hike. He or she doesn't have to go all the way back to the trailhead to start the hike again. That's true for you too. When start doing old or new compulsions, make up your mind to get back on the path at the point where you left off. Pick up where you left off using **actions** to **beat**, **control**, and **defeat** OCD.

Managing Stress

Although the Trickster can return to bother you at any time, it is more likely to come back when you are under stress. Stressors can come from anywhere: family, friends, school, sports, neighbors, and the environment. There is no shortage of stress in our lives. High stress levels can start up your OCD and make it worse. That's why it is so important to take care of yourself and do your best to manage stress. Here are some tried and true buffers for stress that can help you:

- **Realistic thinking:** Looking at situations realistically without exaggerating how threatening or dangerous they are.

- **Mental toughness:** Have a can-do attitude—the belief that you can achieve your goals and cope with problems.

- **Physical fitness:** Exercise and eat well to keep yourself healthy.

- **Social support:** Have family, friends, pets, a therapist, a spiritual advisor, and/or a support group to help you. Offer your support to others.

- **Sense of humor:** Laugh at yourself and try to see the silly side of things.

- **Manage fear and worry:** Practice relaxation skills.

The more buffers you have, the better able you will be to manage your OCD. Check the list to see if you've got enough buffers to help you manage stress. If you don't, then work on adding more. They are **actions** to add to your tool kit.

Enjoy Yourself

There is another very important stress buffer: enjoying your life! A little boy who was tormented by the OCD Trickster said this when he got tired of doing compulsions: "I am just going to enjoy my life!" This is certainly one of the best ways to **beat** OCD!

Now that your OCD is under **control**, do things that you enjoy instead of doing unnecessary compulsions. And be sure to *reward* yourself for all of your hard work! Good luck in your practice of **actions** to **beat**, **control**, and **defeat** OCD! Congratulations Fear Rocket flyer! You have earned your wings!

OCD FEAR ROCKET

Author

Christina J. Taylor, Ph.D. specializes in Cognitive Behavioral Therapy for Anxiety Disorders, including Obsessive Compulsive Disorder, Panic Disorder, Agoraphobia, Social Phobia, Generalized Anxiety Disorder, Specific Phobias, and the OCD spectrum disorder Trichotillomania. Dr. Taylor served for nine years on the Scientific Advisory Board of the National Obsessive Compulsive Foundation and worked on the National Institute of Mental Health Treatment Outcome Study on Panic Disorder at Yale University. She serves on the Scientific Advisory Board of OCD Connecticut. Dr. Taylor lectures widely on Anxiety Disorders and provides training workshops for mental health professionals and consumers on Cognitive Behavioral Therapy. She is a certified Panic Control Therapist and has served as a Clinical Instructor for the Obsessive Compulsive Foundation Behavior Therapy Institute. She appeared on the national television show *20/20 Downtown* as an expert on the treatment of Scrupulosity or "religious" OCD.

Dr. Taylor is an Associate Professor of Psychology at Sacred Heart University in Fairfield, Connecticut. She teaches courses in Abnormal Psychology, Psychopathology, Abnormal Psychology in Film, Psychological Research, the Psychology of Women, and Positive Psychology in Literature and Film.

Online Resources

For your convenience, you may download a PDF version of the worksheets
in this book from our dedicated website: go.pesi.com/OCD

International OCD Foundation
http://iocdf.org

Anxiety and Depression Association of America
http://www.adaa.org/

Fairfield County OCD Support Group
http://fairfieldocdgroup.freehostia.com/index.php.
OCD Connecticut
www.ocdct.org

Obsessive Compulsive Information Center, Madison Institute of Medicine
http://www.miminc.org/aboutocic.asp

Stories About OCD

Hesser, T. S. (1998). *Kissing Doorknobs*. New York: Delacorte Press.
John, B. (2008). *The Boy Who Finally Stopped Washing*. New York: Cooper Union Press.
Kant, J. D. (2008). *The Thought that Counts: A Firsthand Account of One Teenager's Experience with Obsessive Compulsive Disorder*. New York: Oxford University Press.
Niner, H. L. (2004). *Mr. Worry: A Story About OCD*. Morton Grove, Ill: Albert Whitman.

Bibliography

Antony, M. A. & Swinson, R. P. (2009). *When Perfect Isn't Good Enough*. Oakland, CA: New Harbinger Publications.
Ciarrocchi, J. W. (1995). *The Doubting Disease*. Mahwah, NJ: Paulist.
Baer, L. (2001). *The Imp of the Mind*. New York: Dutton.
Chansky, T. (2000). *Freeing Your Child from OCD*. New York: Crown.
Clark, D. A. (2004). *Cognitive Behavioral Therapy for OCD*. New York: Guilford Press.
Fitzgibbons, L. & Pedrick, C. (2003). *Helping Your Child with OCD*. Oakland, CA: New Harbinger Publications.
Freeman, J. B. & Garcia, A. M. (2009). *Family-Based Treatment for Young Children with OCD*. New York: Oxford University Press.
Hyman, B. & Pedrick, C. (2005). *The OCD Workbook: Your Guide to Breaking Free from Obsessive-Compulsive Disorder* (3rd. ed.). Oakland, CA: New Harbinger Publications.
March, J. S. & Benton, C. M. (2007). *Talking Back to OCD*. New York: Guilford Press.
Mumford, P. R. (2004). *Overcoming Compulsive Checking*. Oakland, CA: New Harbinger Publications.
Neziroglu, Bubrick, J., & Yaryura-Tobias, J. A. (2004). *Overcoming Compulsive Hoarding*. Oakland, CA: New Harbinger Publications.
Penzel, F. (2000). *Obsessive-compulsive disorders: A complete guide to getting well and staying well*. New York: Oxford.
Purdon, C. & Clark, D. A. (2005). *Overcoming Obsessive Thoughts*. Oakland, CA: New Harbinger Publications.

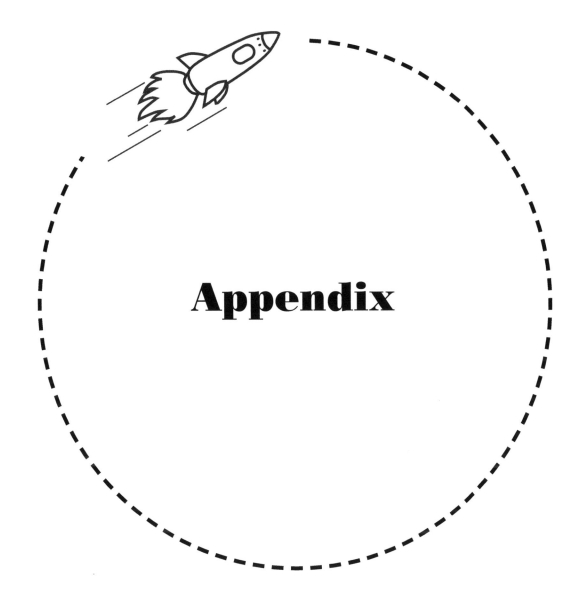

Appendix

My Daily Diary

Fill out this diary every day.

Date & Time	Situation/ Trigger	Obsession: What the Trickster Tells Me to Do	Compulsion: What I Do	How I Would Feel If I Didn't Do The Compulsion – Fear Rocket Rating

Worksheet

My List of Obsessions and Compulsions

#	Obsessions and Compulsions	Fear Rocket Rating

Test and Change Your Thoughts

Situation	My Thoughts - What is Going Through My Head?	How Much I Believe Thought 0-100%	Fear Rocket Rating 1-10	Facts That Support Thought / Facts That Don't Support Thought	Revise How Much I Believe Thought 0-100%	What Is A Realistic Way to Think about The Situation?	Revise Fear Rocket Rating 1-10

Made in the USA
Coppell, TX
29 October 2020